GREAT AMERICAN COOKING SCHOOLS

FOR
JAMES BEARD
AND JULIA CHILD,
WHO LIT THE LAMP
AND SHOWED US
THE WAY

If you would like to
receive a free color
catalog listing all our
books, please send your
name and address to:
Irena Chalmers Cookbooks, Inc.
P.O. Box 988, Denton, NC 27239.

GREAT AMERICAN COOKING SCHOOLS

American Food & California Wine
Bountiful Bread: Basics to Brioches
Christmas Feasts from History
Cooking for Giving
Cooking from a Country Kitchen
Cooking of the South
Dim Sum & Chinese One-Dish Meals
Fair-Game: A Hunter's Cookbook
Fine Fresh Food—Fast
Fresh Garden Vegetables
Ice Cream & Ices
Microwave Cooking: Meals in Minutes
Old-Fashioned Desserts
Omelettes & Soufflés
Pasta! Cooking It, Loving It
Quiche & Pâté
Romantic & Classic Cakes
Soups & Salads
Successful Parties: Simple & Elegant

Cooking for Giving

BERT GREENE & PHILLIP S. SCHULZ

ILLUSTRATED BY SUSAN DAVIS

IRENA CHALMERS COOKBOOKS, INC. • **NEW YORK**

*This book is given with more love than any other gift can convey
to Mildred Schulz, a rare mother and a true friend*

IRENA CHALMERS COOKBOOKS, INC.

PUBLISHER
Irena Chalmers

Managing Editor
Jean Atcheson

Sales and Marketing Director
Diane J. Robbins

Series Design
Helene Berinsky

Cover Design
Milton Glaser
Karen Skelton, *Associate Director*

Cover Photography
Matthew Klein

Designer for this book
Mary Ann Joulwan

Typesetting
Acu-Type Services, Inc., Clinton, CT

Printing
John D. Lucas, Inc., Baltimore, MD

Editorial Office
23 East 92nd Street
New York, NY 10128
(212) 289-3105

Sales Office
P.O. Box 988
Denton, NC 27239
(800) 334-8128 or
(704) 869-4518 (NC)

*The authors tender a deep bow to Judy Blahnik
for her untiring work assembling and testing
most of the recipes in this book. No stove
ever had a more capable third pair of hands.*

ISBN #0-941034-22-4

LIBRARY OF CONGRESS
CATALOG NO.: 84-072216
  Greene, Bert, and Phillip S. Schulz
    Cooking for Giving
  New York, NY: Chalmers, Irena Cookbooks, Inc.
84 p.
E D C B   8 7 6 5   595/19

Contents

Introduction

For the record, this is probably the only cookbook you will ever use that requires one indispensable ingredient in all of its varied recipes: *Love!* For nothing in the collection of homemades that follow, whether it be a jar of gleaming berry jam, a flacon of flavored spirits or a loaf of crusty bread, can be properly whipped up without a healthy measure of affection for the recipient.

That fact established, this book is also a compilation of wonderful pantry items made in limited editions, which are meant to be given as gifts all year long—if you can bear to part with them! It contains some ideas and suggestions about ways of gift-wrapping and methods of presentation, but in this, as in so much else, your own imagination will be your richest resource.

The authors (men of different ages from diverse backgrounds and distant geographies) share a common legacy of their kitchen bequests. Phillip Schulz well remembers his twenty-fifth birthday, the first one spent a continent away from his family home in Colorado, when the best present he received was his mother's "red cake" carefully baked, boxed and wrapped to defy the worst ravages of the postal system, and sent along with detailed instructions for a do-it-yourself duplication of the frosting.

"That cake," Schulz declares, "was like being home again. Better, in fact—because I didn't have to share one slice!"

Bert Greene's recollections of cooking for giving are of a slightly scorched inheritance. When he was a young kid, his mother and grandmother would cautiously circle at least one calendar week per summer as *red-letter canning days.* Unlikely kitchen mates, for both were ladies of independent attitudes, they would become steadfast partners for this sweetly tormenting period, alternately sharing their kitchens for the culinary operation. During that time all other social and familial obligations were put on hold, and children and husband (in Paula Greene's family, at least) were dispatched to a local diner for their meals. Greene's grandmother never went that far, but her family suppers were all cold comforts for the seven days of "jam sessions."

A large black-bladed electric fan would be set up on the Hoosier cabinet to lower the temperature of the kitchen, but it never seemed to make a jot of difference for the fortress of stove and sink literally steamed with pink and purple vapor from morning till night. And those two purposeful women would peel fruit, stir and strain jelly, sterilize jars and cover them with melted paraffin for hours without respite.

What Greene remembers best about those days of strawberry-peach-blueberry-plum-and-grape mania is not the glistening array of jars that filled each woman's jam cellar (it was actually a cabinet of wire mesh that allowed air to circulate about the spoils) but their reluctance to crack open a glassful for their families' consumption.

"This batch is very special," his grandmother would allow, permitting him a taste of the sticky preserves from the leftovers in the pot. "It must be saved for *really* important occasions!" What she actually meant, of course, was *"for really important persons."*

That kind of cooking for giving is a luxury available to precious few in the 1980s. Accordingly, all the largesse in this book has been scaled down to short-term time spans and meant to be prepared by people who, like the authors, lead busy lives. Moreover, every jarred, crocked, tinned and packaged item in the pages that follow is designed to be "put up"—if we may borrow that faintly antique phrase from our forebears—in very restricted kitchen space, using the least amount of effort (and no sweat)!

The bounty is dependent only on the cook's limitless imagination and the recipient's appetite.

So cook up a storm—and add love to taste.

SOME CANNING WISDOM

- Use only prime fruit or vegetables. Clean all the produce thoroughly with a damp cloth, removing any blemishes with a paring knife. Remember, one lackluster berry will sully an entire batch of strawberry jam.
- All canning equipment should be sterilized thoroughly. We boil jars and lids in a large pot, covered by at least an inch of water. Simmer the containers for 15 minutes and then let them stand in hot water. Jars should be inverted on several thicknesses of paper towels to dry. They should always be warm when they are filled and a pair of baby's bottle tongs works wonders in removing them from the hot water. Always use heavy pots made of enameled cast iron or stainless steel for putting up. Aluminum just won't do.
- Always taste what you are making. If the chutney seems bland while it bubbles away on the stove, rest assured it will not improve with age in the jar. But a few drops of vinegar or lemon juice, salt or a speck of sugar will usually perk up any canned comestible.
- When filling jars, a wide-mouthed funnel is essential. Never pack the jars to the very top. Try to allow at least a half-inch between the glass rim and the contents for contraction or expansion. Wipe the jars before sealing so no residual drips will spoil their appearance as gifts later on.
- Sealing a jar means making it *absolutely* airtight. We use screw-top jars with rubber-edged lids. Tighten each jar securely. Never place hot sealed jars in the re-frigerator or in any excessively cool storage place as they may crack when the glass contracts.
- When canning high-acid fruits, it is imperative to give the packed jars a hot-water bath after they are sealed. We give an obligatory soak to everything that is jarred. To do this, place the containers in a large, heavy pot, preferably on a cake rack, or a folded kitchen towel. Add enough hot water to cover the sealed jars by two inches. Slowly bring the water to a boil and simmer for 10 minutes. Extra boiling insures against any spoilage.
- Keep preserved goods in a dark, dry place for a month before using or giving them away. (We save the boxes the Ball jars came in, and repack them to allow the flavors to ripen.)
- Don't worry if (and when) your jar-tops pop. That is just the sound of the jars seal-ing themselves as the preserved goods settle.
- Do worry *a lot*, however, if the lid of a jar buckles, or if your marmalade or con-serves smell fermented. Don't bother to open or taste the stuff, please! Throw it out, immediately.
- Make sure to label all your "put ups" as soon as they are cool to the touch. You can always add a larger, more glamorous label later, superimposed if need be. A good idea is to add another tiny label at the base of the jar listing the date it was canned. Jams, jellies, fruit butters, marmalades and conserves all have a shelf life of one year at best.

Cocktail Nibbles

C rispy hors d'oeuvres cover a wide latitude and serve an obvious common purpose: to keep drinkers occupied so they don't imbibe too much too soon.

We abhor most packaged varieties of such "fly-foods"—known as such because they are always wolfed down on the fly. They are almost invariably oversalted and overgreasy for one thing, and chock-full of unhealthful and nasty chemical preservatives for another.

In our opinion the best cocktail nibbles are usually toasted or roasted and seasoned with judgment rather than an unrestrained salt shaker. Consider the following collection as a case in point. Each can be made in less than an hour—and kept indefinitely (jarred) in a cool cupboard or freezer. Keep an eye out for appropriate gift containers. We have packed ours in antique crocks, contemporary kitchen canisters, and even foil-lined Mexican clay pots—all topped with ruffs of cellophane and ribbon. Very special recipients get a card, handsomely inscribed with the recipe.

Peppered Peanuts

It is, to be sure, more economical to buy unshelled peanuts for the following recipe, but since we never seem to have the time to roast our own, we end up with the packaged store-bought ones. Serve these as soon as they cool down; if they have been stored cool or frozen, reheat them before serving.

1½ tablespoons vegetable oil
2 cloves garlic, finely chopped
2 cups salted, dry-roasted peanuts
4 teaspoons ground dried chilies
(mild to hot, according to taste)
or chili powder
½ teaspoon freshly ground pepper

Heat the oil in a large heavy cast-iron skillet until very hot, but not smoking. Stir in the garlic, peanuts and chilies. Cook, stirring constantly, for 4 minutes. Stir in the ground pepper. Remove from the heat. Transfer with a slotted spoon to paper towels and pat dry.

The nuts can be eaten as soon as they have cooled. To give immediately, we put them in a decorative tin with a tightly fitting lid. If you want to keep them on hand, pack the cooled nuts into a sterilized jar, seal and store in a cool place for up to 3 weeks.

Garlicky Pecans

There is no man (woman or child) with active taste buds who can resist the savor of a toasted or roasted pecan. Coat the crunchy nuts with spices and garlic, and you have a drinking companion that cannot be beat. Pack the nuts into a glass jar with a tight-fitting lid. Add a bright bow and a brighter hang-tag inscribed with the recipe. Make sure to note, however, that leftovers may be frozen in airtight bags and thawed again at room temperature.

1 tablespoon unsalted butter
2 teaspoons hot pepper sauce
3 cloves garlic, crushed
2 tablespoons soy sauce
1 pound pecan halves
¼ teaspoon crushed dried hot red
peppers
1 tablespoon seasoned pepper
Salt

Preheat the oven to 350 degrees.

Butter a baking sheet liberally and sprinkle it with the hot pepper sauce, garlic and soy sauce. Distribute the pecans evenly over the sheet and stir with a fork until they are well coated with the seasonings. Sprinkle with crushed hot peppers, 1½ teaspoons of pepper and salt to taste. Bake in the preheated oven for 10 minutes.

Sprinkle the pecans with the remaining pepper and more salt. Stir with a fork; bake 15 minutes longer. Cool in pan on a rack. To keep, freeze in airtight bags, or pack into sterilized jars, seal and store in a cool place for up to 3 weeks.

Spicy Macadamias

Makes ½ pound

Hawaiian macadamias are toothsome at any hour of the day, but they become super party fare when the bland kernels are spiked with hot pepper and herbs. Store a batch of these in the freezer and simply reheat in a warm oven (for five minutes) whenever a doorbell announces unexpected guests at cocktail time.

Vegetable oil
2 small cloves garlic, crushed
1 teaspoon crushed, dried hot red peppers
1½ teaspoons seasoned salt
1½ teaspoons seasoned pepper
2 teaspoons chili powder
¼ teaspoon cayenne pepper
¼ teaspoon paprika
½ pound macadamia nuts
1½ teaspoons unsalted butter

Rub a heavy skillet with oil and place over moderate heat. Add the garlic and seasonings. Stir briefly; add the macadamia nuts and butter. Reduce the heat to low. Stir until the nuts are coated with the mixture, adding more butter if necessary. Cool in pan on a rack. Store in an airtight container. These nuts will keep for several weeks in the refrigerator—longer in the freezer. We often package them in airtight plastic-lidded "store & see" clear glass jars that are handsome as the dickens.

Curried Sunflower Seeds

Makes 1½ pints

Sunflower seeds are addictive—straight off the blossoms on the backyard fence. Zapping the crunchy kernels with curry powder and turmeric gives them a golden glow and turns a natural health food into an irresistible cocktail hors d'oeuvre. Try stopping after just one handful! For a gift container, cover an everyday kitchen tin with a plastic lid (baking powder, or small shortening can, etc.) with leftover scraps of brightly colored fabric or wallpaper.

2 tablespoons unsalted butter
1 clove garlic, crushed
2 teaspoons curry powder
½ teaspoon ground turmeric
1 pound raw hulled sunflower seeds, unsalted
Salt and freshly ground pepper

Heat the butter in a heavy skillet over moderate heat, add the garlic, curry powder and turmeric, and whisk until smooth. Add the sunflower seeds; stir with a wooden spoon until they are well coated, about 2 minutes. Add salt and pepper to taste. Allow the mixture to cool. Pack into sterilized jars or airtight gift containers. Store in the refrigerator for up to 2 weeks.

Barbecued Cashews

Makes about 1½ pints

The barbecue sauce is the most important element of this recipe. We suggest using leftover home-made "stuff" that you will find in the section on Sauces, but any good commercially available sauce will do. Cork-topped wide-mouthed jars make attractive gift containers.

2 teaspoons unsalted butter
6 tablespoons barbecue sauce
2 tablespoons ketchup
3 tablespoons brown sugar
1 teaspoon ground allspice
1 teaspoon mild ground chilies
⅛ teaspoon hot pepper sauce
14 ounces dry-roasted cashews
Freshly ground pepper

Preheat the oven to 400 degrees.

Rub a baking sheet with the butter. Combine the barbecue sauce, ketchup, brown sugar, allspice, ground chilies and hot pepper sauce in a bowl and mix thoroughly. Brush the mixture over the baking sheet; place in the oven for 1 minute.

Sprinkle the cashews over the prepared baking sheet; toss and stir until well coated with the mixture. Sprinkle with pepper, to taste.

Reduce the oven temperature to 350 degrees. Bake the cashews in the oven, stirring once, until nicely browned, about 8 minutes. Cool in the pan on a rack. Store in an airtight container in the refrigerator. These nuts will keep for about 1 week.

Cheese Sticks

This recipe is a talisman. It was an invention of the late Michael Field, a giant in the food field, who was also responsible for discovering Bert Greene cooking up a storm at The Store in Amagansett in the early 1960s. Michael gave Bert the following recipe (from his book All Manner of Food, *Knopf, 1965) with a grace note: "To alter the flavor of these fragile crisps somewhat, stir 1 or 2 teaspoons of sesame, caraway, poppy seeds, or cracked black pepper, into the dough before you add the egg yolk and water mixture."*

4 tablespoons unsalted butter, chilled and cut into bits
⅓ cup finely grated aged sharp cheddar cheese
3 tablespoons freshly grated Parmesan cheese
1 cup flour
½ teaspoon cayenne pepper
1 egg yolk
2 tablespoons iced water

Combine the butter bits, cheese, flour and cayenne pepper in a mixing bowl; toss them about with your fingers. Then rub them together until they blend and look like flakes of coarse meal. The dough should remain fairly dry; don't overmix or it will become oily.

Combine the egg yolk and water in a small bowl; beat lightly with a fork. Pour the mixture over the dough and toss together with your fingers or a fork until it can be gathered into a compact ball. Wrap in wax paper and refrigerate for 1 hour.

Preheat the oven to 400 degrees.

Flour a working surface lightly and roll the dough into a rectangle approximately 4 by 15 inches. Trim the edges of the rectangle with a sharp knife or pastry wheel and cut the pastry crosswise into strips 4 inches long by ½ inch wide. Transfer the strips with a spatula to 1 or 2 ungreased baking sheets. Bake in the center of the preheated oven until the sticks are firm to the touch, about 10 minutes. Be careful not to let them brown. Cool the sticks on a wire rack.

Pack in decorative airtight tins and store in the refrigerator until ready to give. These straws taste best at room temperature, so let them stand at least 20 minutes after removing from the refrigerator.

Olives Vinaigrette

Makes about 1 pint

This recipe is a Greene/Schulz culinary brainstorm, devised (after a party) when the hosts discovered a mess of leftover black olives and an equal excess of vinaigrette sauce. We decided to combine both in a Ball jar and these highly seasoned olives are the happy result.

This gift is a double-barreled donation. The recipient may serve up the olives on a canape tray and husband the vinaigrette sauce to splash over a green salad later on. If you like, offer the canape tray (or a salad bowl) along with an attractive glass jar of these olives.

1¾ to 2 cups pitted black olives
2 large cloves garlic, crushed
1 teaspoon coarse salt
1 tablespoon Dijon mustard
2 teaspoons lemon juice
4 teaspoons red wine vinegar
⅔ cup olive oil
1 teaspoon freshly ground pepper

Place the olives in a sterilized pint container, or in 2 half-pint containers.

Mash the garlic with the salt in a small bowl until smooth. Whisk in the mustard, lemon juice, vinegar and oil. Add pepper to taste. Pour the mixture over the olives. Seal the containers and store in the refrigerator.

Shrimp Seviche

Makes about 1½ quarts

Peruvians have a tradition of combining tomatoes with citrus juice to cure and season fish. One of the more bracing of their innovations is the following zesty hors d'oeuvre. We often pack seviche in fancy see-through jars with wire closures, but any pleasing glass or ceramic container will do.

1 pound uncooked shrimp,
  shelled and deveined
1 cup freshly squeezed lime juice
¼ cup chopped shallots
1 clove garlic, finely chopped
¼ cup chopped parsley
1 small tomato, peeled, seeded,
  cut into strips
3 tablespoons finely chopped
  green chili peppers
1½ teaspoons salt
1 teaspoon freshly ground pepper
Dash of hot pepper sauce
¼ cup chopped fresh coriander
½ cup olive oil

Combine all the ingredients in a large bowl and mix thoroughly. Pack into sterilized airtight containers or jars and seal. Refrigerate the seviche for at least 12 hours before using, and store, refrigerated. Seviche will hold for about 5 days.

Spreads & Pâtés

In our grandparents' time, a "spread" inevitably implied a collation of grand and glorious foods that took days to make and hours to consume. Nowadays a *spread* has a somewhat more colloquial ring, denoting the one item on a cocktail tray that has been either crocked or potted (therapeutically) to keep party guests from becoming crocked or potted themselves!

Spreads (as the name indicates) are usually a soft-natured upholstery meant to enhance crispy crackers or warm fingers of toast. And no party (or party-giver for that matter) should be without a jar stashed away for emergencies. And that is where cooking for giving comes in.

Pâtés, on quite the other hand, are seriously solid assets meant to be sliced for buffet suppers or picnic sandwiches as the occasion arises. Time was, everyone believed that pâté was either impossibly rich, improbably expensive or awesomely hard to prepare. Nothing could be further from the truth, however, as any practiced hand at the processor will attest.

All these pâtés and spreads may be prepared, refrigerated or frozen well in advance of giving. Their appeal is, of course, greatly enhanced by really attractive containers. French onion soup bowls (with lids) and covered terrines make elegant receptacles, but even sculpted unglazed ceramic flower pots will serve in a pinch. But do make certain they are properly cured (or line them with foil first) as low-fired clay will sometimes contaminate foodstuffs.

Wrap the tops of all crocked items well in several layers of plastic wrap and foil, to retard spoilage, before embellishing them with cellophane and ribbons. And remember to note the shelf life of your gift on an accompanying card for extra social security.

Olive Butter

One of the most tonic spreads we know (a deep black olive butter) is sometimes known as "poor man's caviar" because it is almost as good and costs a fraction of the price. This dish (Russians call it Tamar) may be prepared at least two weeks prior to giving, if the crock is really well sealed to prevent contamination from any random refrigerator odors. After we seal the crocks, we generally tie a square of brightly colored fabric over the top.

1 large can pitted black olives,
   drained thoroughly
1 large clove garlic
2 shallots
12 ounces unsalted butter,
   at room temperature
Dash hot pepper sauce
½ teaspoon lemon juice
½ teaspoon salt
Freshly ground pepper

Combine the olives, garlic and shallots in the container of a food processor or blender; puree until smooth. Transfer to a wire sieve and allow all the liquid to drain off.

Whip the butter in a large bowl until it is light and creamy. Gradually add the olive puree. Beat until the mixture is a light gray color, similar to caviar. Add the hot pepper sauce, lemon juice, salt and pepper to taste. Pack into an airtight earthenware crock. Refrigerate.

Potted Shrimp

Nothing could be more soothing with martinis than this English classic when combined with a stack of good dark bread. If fresh tiny shrimp are not locally available, use larger shrimp and chop them once they are cooked. We have tried using the frozen kind but found them lacking in taste.

2 cups cooked tiny shrimp,
   deveined and shelled
½ cup lemon juice
1 cup unsalted butter, softened
2 tablespoons snipped fresh dill
2 teaspoons finely chopped
   anchovy fillets
¼ teaspoon salt
Pinch cayenne pepper
1 tablespoon coarsely ground
   black pepper

Combine shrimp and lemon juice in a small bowl. Let stand covered at room temperature for 1 hour. Drain.

Cream the butter in a large mixing bowl. Beat in the snipped dill, anchovies, salt and cayenne pepper. Fold in the shrimp; taste and adjust seasonings.

Spoon the shrimp mixture into a small earthenware crock or ceramic mug. Sprinkle the top with black pepper. Cover and refrigerate for at least 5 hours. Store in the refrigerator.

Peppered Veal Terrine

Makes a 1½-quart terrine

A wondrously peppery meatloaf will have your "hot"-loving friends clamoring for more. (Eating it is also a great way of clearing the sinuses.) Note on the tag that it can be served slightly warmed, or cold. A crusty loaf of bread is a good secondary gift.

Butter, to grease the terrine
2 pounds ground veal
3 stalks celery, chopped
½ cup finely chopped parsley
½ cup strong chicken broth
¼ cup peppercorns, crushed
½ cup breadcrumbs
1 egg, lightly beaten
½ teaspoon salt
2 strips bacon

Preheat the oven to 350 degrees. Butter a 1½-quart terrine.

Place the meat in a large mixing bowl. Combine the celery, parsley, and chicken broth in the container of a food processor or blender; process or blend until pureed.

Add the vegetable puree, peppercorns, breadcrumbs, egg and salt to the meat and mix thoroughly.

Pack the mixture into the terrine and lay the bacon strips on top. Bake, uncovered, in the preheated oven for 1½ hours. Pour off the excess liquids and allow to cool. Cover, and refrigerate.

NOTE: Tightly covered, the terrine will keep in the refrigerator for up to 10 days.

To prepare it for giving, cut a circle or oval of plastic wrap 2 inches beyond the width of the top of the terrine. Place the piece of plastic wrap over the top, stretch it taut and secure with twine or tape. Put the lid on the terrine and tie it in place with gaily colored ribbon.

Spinach and Tuna Terrine

Makes a 1½-quart terrine

Like the previous recipe, this seafood-spinach pâté can be served directly from the terrine in which it is given. It can also be sliced thinly and served with lemony mayonnaise. This dish will keep for 3 or 4 days, well refrigerated. A handsome (ovenproof) receptacle will make the gift even more lavish.

Butter, to grease the terrine
2 10-ounce packages frozen
    chopped spinach
⅓ cup unblanched almonds
4-ounce can tuna, drained, flaked
    with a fork (about ½ cup)
3 anchovy fillets
½ teaspoon capers
½ cup peeled shallots
1 small clove garlic, chopped
3 eggs
¾ cup heavy cream
1 tablespoon lemon juice
1 teaspoon finely grated
    lemon rind
⅛ teaspoon freshly grated nutmeg
Dash of hot pepper sauce
Salt and freshly ground pepper
2 ounces smoked salmon,
    thinly sliced
3 tablespoons sliced pimientos
5 or 6 imported black olives (we
    prefer Calamatas in olive oil),
    drained, sliced from pits

Preheat the oven to 375 degrees. Butter a 1½-quart terrine.

Cook the spinach in boiling salted water until completely defrosted, about 2 minutes. Drain through a sieve, pressing out all the liquid with the back of a spoon. Transfer to a large mixing bowl.

Place the almonds in the container of a blender or food processor and blend at high speed until pulverized. Add the tuna, anchovy fillets, capers, shallots, garlic, eggs and cream, and blend until smooth. Combine the almond-tuna mixture with the spinach. Add the lemon juice, lemon rind, nutmeg, hot pepper sauce and salt and pepper to taste. Mix thoroughly.

Layer one-third of the mixture in the bottom of the terrine. Cover with smoked salmon slices. Add another layer of spinach mixture. Arrange 2 tablespoons of pimientos alternately with olive slices over the top. Cover with the remaining spinach mixture and make a design with the remaining pimientos around the edges.

Cover the terrine with aluminum foil and place in a roasting pan. Pour enough boiling water into the pan to reach about halfway up the sides of the terrine. Bake in the preheated oven until a knife inserted in the center comes out fairly clean, about 1 hour.

Remove the terrine from the water bath and cool on a rack to room temperature. Cover tightly, and refrigerate for at least 6 hours.

To prepare for giving, cut a circle or oval of plastic wrap 2 inches beyond the width of the top of the terrine. Place the piece of plastic wrap over the top, stretch it taut and secure with twine or tape. Put the lid on the terrine and tie it in place with striped ribbon.

Devilled Ham

Makes about 1½ pints

Nothing in the world beats homemade devilled ham. What makes this spread so satiny/satanic is the blending of sweet butter, good mustard and minced jalapeños. We pack ours into a glazed pottery jar, and add a written tag to ensure that the one who receives it serves this exquisite sandwich filling at room temperature on fresh, warm bread. If it's appropriate, you could add your own newly baked loaf to the presentation.

1 pound cooked ham, finely chopped
2 canned jalapeño peppers, finely chopped
6 tablespoons unsalted butter, softened
2 teaspoons Dijon mustard
Salt and freshly ground black pepper

Combine the ham, jalapeño peppers, butter and mustard in a bowl and mash them into a paste with a heavy wooden spoon. (This may also be done in a food processor.) Add salt and pepper to taste. Pack the mixture into a sterilized jar or airtight crock. Store refrigerated.

Pâté of Pot Roast

Makes about 2 pints

There are pâtés and PÂTÉS. One of the easiest (and most satisfying) to make is a savory hors d'oeuvre devised from leftover pot roast. This makes a great bread-and-butter gift done up in a rustic country napkin, with a loaf of bread to accompany it. The best thing about buttery pâtés is that they last (well sealed) in the refrigerator—and, believe it or not, the flavor of this one improves as it ages.

2 cups coarsely chopped cold pot roast, trimmed of all fat and gristle
8 anchovy fillets, drained, washed and dried
¾ cup strong beef broth
8 ounces unsalted butter, softened
1 tablespoon finely grated onion
1 shallot, finely chopped
1 clove garlic, crushed
Dash of hot pepper sauce
1 teaspoon lemon juice
½ teaspoon salt
Freshly ground black pepper

Combine the pot roast, anchovies and beef stock in the container of a food processor or blender. Process at high speed, stopping often to scrape the sides with a rubber spatula and adding more stock if necessary until the puree is smooth and fairly fluid. Transfer to a sieve. Force the puree through the sieve with the back of a large spoon to produce as smooth a paste as possible.

Beat the butter in a bowl until it is smooth and light in color. Add the butter to the meat puree, 1 tablespoonful at a time, beating the puree after each addition until the butter and meat are completely combined. Add the onion, shallot, garlic, hot pepper sauce, lemon juice, salt and pepper to taste.

Spoon into an earthenware crock and chill for at least 4 hours. Store, covered, in the refrigerator.

Soups

A gift meant to be sipped (hot or cold) is appropriate in any season of the year. We prefer to give most soups *frozen* in an airtight quart container because the solid state allows the recipient a measure of independence about when and where it is to be served. However, the most thoughtful house-warming gift (or offering to a convalescent) in our repertoire is always a wide-mouthed thermos of some bracing chowder or velvety pottage, meant to be consumed the very moment the donor departs.

The range of soups at a gift-giver's command is endless. We have simply chosen some that dinner companions over the year request most often.

One soup-gift story is worth telling. A young bride of our acquaintance begged us for "no wedding presents, please . . . except those that can be warmed up!" For the poor girl, a novice in the kitchen, did not wish to waste the first precious days of her married life adrift in a sea of Campbell's and Heinz. Taking her literally at her word, we gave her six utterly tantalizing containers of frozen soup plus a handsome ceramic-over-cast-iron soup pot to warm them up in. This couple has apparently lived happily ever after, so the soup-maker/gift-givers may perhaps take a jot of credit. Oh yes, we included six loaves of homemade (frozen) bread as part of her K-rations.

Pflaumenüs

Makes about 1½ quarts

Pflaumenüs is a soup with a funny history to its moniker. Bert Greene found the recipe in a Mennonite church bulletin (at a garage sale in Topeka, Kansas) and published it as it was misprinted (in 1850) as pflaumenüs. He corrected the spelling only after it was pointed out by a higher authority that pflaumen means plum in German. Give it, well sealed with plastic wrap, in a pretty covered bowl. Shelf life: 1 week in the refrigerator. In the freezer: 6 months.

2 16-ounce cans purple plums in heavy syrup
½ cup finely chopped rhubarb
⅔ cup granulated sugar
1 cup water
½ cup dry red wine
¼ teaspoon ground white pepper
Pinch of salt
½ teaspoon grated lemon peel
1 tablespoon lemon juice
1 cinnamon stick
½ cup whipping cream
1 tablespoon cornstarch
3 tablespoons brandy
1 cup sour cream

Drain the plums and reserve the syrup. Remove the pits and chop the plums into small pieces. Place chopped plums in a medium-sized saucepan. Add the reserved syrup, the rhubarb, sugar, water, wine, white pepper, salt, lemon peel, lemon juice and cinnamon stick. Bring to a boil; reduce the heat, and simmer 15 minutes. Add the whipping cream and simmer 5 more minutes. Discard the cinnamon stick.

Mix the cornstarch and brandy until smooth and add to the soup, stirring slowly. Cook until the soup has thickened slightly. Remove from the heat.

Combine 1 cup sour cream with 1 cup soup in a small bowl; mix thoroughly. Slowly stir this mixture back into the soup; mix well. Let the soup cool. Pour into a wide-mouthed plastic container or jar and cover or seal tightly. Chill thoroughly. Store in the refrigerator.

Carrot Vichyssoise

Makes 1 to 1½ quarts

Consider giving this soup in a tall attractive pitcher surrounded with six mugs. A mushroom basket (with a handle) makes for easy carrying. Be sure to wrap the top of the pitcher securely with plastic wrap, before covering it with fabric and tying it in place with a ribbon.

2 cups peeled, chopped potatoes
(about 2 medium-size)
1¼ cups chopped carrots (about
3 medium-size)
6 scallions (white part only),
chopped
3 cups chicken broth
⅛ teaspoon white pepper
½ teaspoon freshly grated nutmeg
1¼ cups whipping cream
Salt

Place the potatoes, carrots, scallions and chicken broth in a saucepan; bring to a boil. Reduce the heat; simmer until the vegetables are tender, about 20 to 25 minutes.

Transfer the mixture to a blender container or food processor bowl, half at a time; blend until smooth, taking care not to overfill the container as the hot liquid will splash up. Pour the soup into a large bowl.

Stir white pepper, nutmeg, cream and salt to taste into soup. Pour into a wide-mouthed plastic container or jar. Cover, and chill at least 4 hours. Store in the refrigerator until ready to give. Shelf life: 3 to 4 days, maximum.

Mushroom, Barley, Tomato Soup

Makes about 2 quarts

This ethnic, though totally American, soup is of Jewish-Polish-Rumanian-Russian background, and a family inheritance of the Greenes. It can be given in an ovenproof crock for easy reheating, or presented in a wide-mouthed thermos with a loaf of gaily wrapped bread and a crock of sweet butter. Shelf life: 2 to 3 weeks in the refrigerator; longer in the freezer.

2 tablespoons vegetable oil
1¼ pounds stewing beef, cut
into 1-inch cubes
1 clove garlic
5 cups water
½ cup boiling water
½ ounce dried, sliced mushrooms
1 small onion, chopped
1 carrot, chopped
¾ cup chopped celery, including
root end
1 cup chopped, seeded, peeled
tomatoes
½ teaspoon granulated sugar
1 small parsnip, chopped
1 small white turnip, chopped
Pinch of dried thyme
¼ cup barley
4 cups beef broth (approximately)
Salt and freshly ground pepper,
to taste

Heat the oil in a large, heavy saucepan or Dutch oven over high heat. Add the meat; sauté until well browned on all sides. Add the garlic and 4 cups water; stir, scraping the bottom and sides of the pot. Bring to a boil; reduce the heat, and simmer, partially covered, for 1 hour. Remove fatty residue as it rises to the surface. Discard garlic.

Pour ½ cup boiling water over the mushrooms in a small bowl. Let stand at least 20 minutes.

Add the mushrooms with liquid to the soup. Add the onion, carrot, celery, tomatoes, sugar, parsnip, turnip, thyme, barley, beef broth and the remaining 1 cup water. Simmer, partially covered, until the meat is tender, about 1¼ hours. If the soup becomes too thick, thin it with more beef broth. Season to taste with salt and pepper.

Pour into a wide-mouthed plastic container or jar. Seal, and store in the refrigerator until ready to reheat. A wide-mouthed thermos can be wrapped in a tea towel for a jaunty presentation.

Black Bean Soup

Another candidate to fill an attractive ovenproof dish is this Puerto Rican black bean soup. It is traditional to serve this soup with a garnish, so we affix a label to the crock: "Serve with the following garnishes: finely chopped cooked ham, chopped scallions, chopped hard-cooked egg, thinly sliced lime, cooked rice." This is another soup that freezes well. Shelf life: 2 to 3 weeks in the refrigerator; longer in the freezer.

1 pound black turtle beans
⅓ cup diced salt pork
2 tablespoons olive oil
½ cup diced cooked ham
2 medium-size onions, chopped
2 cloves garlic, finely chopped
8 cups beef broth
8 cups water
1 large bay leaf
1 small onion, studded with
  2 cloves
1 small sprig fresh oregano or
  a pinch of dried
Pinch of cayenne pepper
2 teaspoons wine vinegar
2 tablespoons sherry
Salt and freshly ground pepper,
  to taste

Sort through the beans; soak in cold water overnight. Drain.

Drop the salt pork into a pan of boiling water; boil 5 minutes. Drain and pat dry with paper towels.

Heat the oil in a large, heavy pot over moderate heat; add the salt pork and diced ham. Cook, stirring constantly, for 8 minutes. Add chopped onions and garlic; cook 5 minutes longer.

Stir in the beans, beef broth, 4 cups of the water, the bay leaf, onion studded with cloves, and oregano. Bring to a boil; reduce heat. Cook over moderate heat, stirring occasionally, for 1½ hours. Add the remaining water as the liquid begins to reduce.

When the beans are tender, remove three-fifths of them with a slotted spoon. Place, in two batches, in a blender container or food processor bowl. Add some soup liquid and blend until smooth. Stir both batches back into the soup. Discard the onion and bay leaf.

Add the cayenne pepper, vinegar, sherry, and salt and pepper to taste. Cook over moderate heat until the soup becomes quite thick, about 30 minutes. Pour into a wide-mouthed plastic container and freeze, or pour into an attractive jar or ovenproof pot. Cover or seal tightly, and store in the refrigerator until ready to reheat.

Chutneys & Relishes

In the authors' prejudiced opinion, there are two condiments no self-respecting refrigerator should ever be without: *chutney* and *relish*.

Chutney (it comes from the Hindu word *catni*) literally means: to taste. It's an apt translation, for in our culinary experience, nothing heightens a strong-flavored dish (such as Vindaloo curry) or enhances a mild one (such as chicken salad) or intensifies a creamy one (such as clam pie) more effectively than a dab of chutney.

Rumor has it that the first European to realize the savory virtue of this tart sauce was a major in the Bengal Lancers named Grey, who evolved a seasoning to mask the indifferent taste and less than fresh texture of the Indian meats being served to his troops in the mid-19th-century heyday of the British raj. His sauce was composed of what nature and the Bengal landscape had most to offer: mangoes, peppers and spices. Major Grey never copyrighted his invention, and while it is now common culinary currency all over the world, his heirs never shared in its popularity.

Relish made an even earlier appearance (the English word was first noted in 1798, borrowed from the Old French word *reles*, which means: something remaining). If you think this implies that relish peps up a left-over, you are right on target. It will also enliven a sandwich, salad, roast or rollmop, and even lend dignity to a hot dog. Relishes vary as to ingredients; the best of ours are alternately vegetable- or fruit-based. All, like the chutneys that precede them, make handsome gifts (in sterilized jars, please!).

Chutneys and relishes too, though well sluiced with vinegar for staying power, are not harmed (and probably augmented for the better) by a 10- to 15-minute hot-water bath once they are packed and sealed. Add your own labels and tags afterwards, to avoid any possibility of blurring water spots.

New Orleans-Style Fruit Chutney

Makes about 3 pints

From the rich bounty of Creole cookery comes the following tangy fruit chutney, whose recipe is such an old and family-kept secret that it was passed down by word of mouth alone. The canny authors, in fact, had to rush away from the prescription-giver and make notes instantly. Every time we make it, this chutney changes slightly (for the fruit is always a mite riper or a touch drier) but the texture and essential flavor always remain dark and delectably rich.

½ **pineapple, peeled, cored, cut into 1¼-inch chunks (about 1¾ cups)**
2 **pears, peeled, cored and sliced**
Pulp from ½ large orange
¼ **cup orange juice**
1 **small mango (about 6 ounces)**
¾ **cup dark brown sugar, packed**
4 **ounces dried figs, cut into pieces**
¼ **cup raisins**
4 **dried apricots**
Finely slivered rind from ½ lemon
Finely slivered rind from ½ orange
1½ **teaspoons candied ginger, cut into strips**
½ **teaspoon ground mace**
1 **cinnamon stick broken in half**
¾ **cup walnut meats**
½ **cup grated coconut**
1½ **teaspoons vinegar**
¾ **cup dark rum (approximately)**

Combine the fresh fruits, juice and sugar in a medium-sized saucepan. Bring to a boil, reduce the heat and simmer for 5 minutes. Add the dried fruits, orange and lemon rinds, ginger, mace and cinnamon. Simmer for 30 minutes.

Add the walnuts, coconut and vinegar. Continue to cook until all the fruit is soft. Add the rum; bring to just under the boil. Remove from the heat.

Spoon into hot sterilized jars, seal, and store in a cool place for several months. Or cool and place in any covered glass container and keep in the refrigerator for 2 to 3 weeks.

Green Tomato Chutney

Makes 2½ pints

If you are lucky enough to have a garden, or a farmer's market nearby, September is the time for green tomatoes. Next time you have a batch on hand, give this extra-special chutney a whirl.

½ lemon
1 teaspoon mustard seed
½ cinnamon stick
2½ cups chopped peeled green
    tomatoes (about 1½ pounds)
2 red peppers, seeded, cut
    into strips
1½ cups chopped green apples,
    peeled and cored
1 cup plus 2 tablespoons
    brown sugar, packed
1 cup cider vinegar
¾ cup dark raisins
½ cup chopped dates
½ cup chopped onions
¼ cup diced crystallized
    ginger
½ or 1 small dried red chili
    pepper, crushed
1 teaspoon salt
½ clove garlic, finely chopped
⅛ teaspoon cayenne pepper
Pinch ground allspice
Pinch ground cloves
½ cup chopped walnuts
2 tablespoons pimiento strips

Pare the zest (the colored part of the peel) from the lemon and cut it into slivers. Remove and discard the white pith from the lemon; chop the pulp; discard the pits. Tie the mustard seeds and cinnamon in cheesecloth. Combine the lemon zest, pulp, spice bag and all the remaining ingredients except the nuts and pimiento in a large saucepan and bring to a boil. Reduce the heat and simmer, uncovered, stirring frequently, until thick, about 2½ hours. Stir in the nuts; cook 10 minutes. Stir in the pimiento; remove and discard the spice bag. Pack the chutney into hot sterilized jars, leaving ½ inch head space. Seal. Place in a hot-water bath for 10 minutes. Store in a cool place.

Corn Relish

Makes about 4 pints

For good reason, we have a hard time keeping this one on hand. Best when made in late August, this relish gets given away so fast that you may want to make a few extra jars for yourself. The original formula came from Iowa and was rumored to have once taken a blue ribbon at the state fair.

2½ cups raw corn, cut from
    the cob
2½ cups chopped raw cabbage
    (about 1 small cabbage)
3 medium-size yellow onions,
    finely chopped
2 medium-size red peppers,
    seeded, chopped
1 large green pepper, seeded,
    chopped
1 ounce dry mustard
1½ teaspoons celery seed
¾ teaspoon turmeric
1½ tablespoons salt
¾ cup brown sugar
2 cups vinegar

Combine all the ingredients in a large saucepan. Bring to a boil and simmer, stirring often, for 1 hour. Pour into hot sterilized jars. Seal. Place in a hot-water bath for 10 minutes. Store in a cool place or in the refrigerator.

(Jar collectors seek out unusual "oldies" at tag and garage sales. Always seal them well with paraffin wax.)

Ruby Apple Relish

Makes about 2 pints

The bonus of this crimson table pleaser, frankly, is its ease of production. We timed it in the kitchen— and put up six pints in a half-hour (including the sterilizing of jars). Now that's quick cookery!

2 green apples (Greenings or
    Granny Smith), peeled, cored
    and quartered
Juice of 1 lemon
Slivered rind of 1 lemon
Pulp and juice of 1 orange
Slivered rind of 1 orange
12-ounce package cranberries,
    washed and picked over
1 cup superfine sugar
¼ cup apple brandy or apple
    schnapps (optional)

Place the apples in the container of a food processor or blender. Sprinkle with lemon juice, lemon peel, orange juice and pulp, and the orange peel. Using the pulse button, or on/off motion, process the apples until they are finely chopped. Transfer to a bowl.

Place the cranberries in the container of the food processor. Add the sugar and brandy, if using, and process, as before, until finely chopped. Add the cranberries to the apple mixture; mix thoroughly. Spoon into sterilized jars, seal and store in the refrigerator.

NOTE: The relish will keep in airtight containers for up to 4 weeks.

Red Relish

A recipe inspired by Phillip Schulz's sister Linda Herbert (see page 38), this red relish can turn a hot dog into haute cuisine. Linda salts hers and lets it stand overnight, draining it the next day. Because we cook it quickly, a lot of juice accumulates in the pot, so it is necessary to strain the mixture before putting it into jars. Being thrifty in the kitchen, however, we turn the excess liquid into a hot-pepper sauce (recipe follows). Voila! Two recipes in one.

3 medium-size onions, peeled
3 medium-size zucchini, trimmed
3 large green peppers, seeded
2 medium-size red peppers,
** seeded**
2 medium-size underripe (firm)
** tomatoes**
1 cup granulated sugar
2 teaspoons mustard seed
2 teaspoons celery seed
½ teaspoon ground turmeric
1 cup cider vinegar

Shred the onions, zucchini, peppers and tomatoes, using the shredding blade of a food processor. Place the shredded vegetables in a large heavy saucepan and add the remaining ingredients. Bring to a boil; boil for 4 minutes.

Using a slotted spoon, pack the relish into hot sterilized jars. (Reserve the excess liquid.) Seal the jars and place in a hot-water bath for 10 minutes. Store in a cool place.

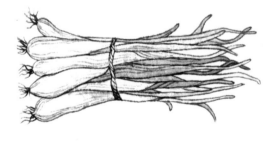

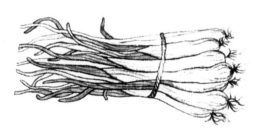

Spicy Red Sauce

This sauce is excellent in salad dressings and wonderful on fruit. We give it away in small bottles with regular screw-cap lids.

Strained liquid reserved from
** Red Relish (about 1½ cups)**
½ teaspoon hot pepper sauce, or
** to taste**

Combine the liquid from the relish with the hot pepper sauce. Pour into hot sterilized bottles. Seal. Store in the refrigerator.

Cranberry-Mango Relish

Cranberry and mango are the components of the most heavenly hash we have ever sampled. Neither sweet nor tart, it is the perfectly tempered flavoring to add distinction to a roast of beef or a rack of lamb.

**12-ounce package fresh
 cranberries
1 cup granulated sugar
Seeded pulp of 2 oranges
Seeded pulp of 2 limes
2 mangoes, peeled and sliced**

Combine all the ingredients in the container of a food processor or blender. Pulse the machine on and off several times quickly until the sugar is dissolved and the fruit is roughly chopped. Spoon into hot sterilized jars, seal and refrigerate.

Chow Chow

Chow chow is an old-fashioned Midwestern palate perker, served at church suppers, Lodge picnics and Sunday nights when relatives dropped in. The tang of mustard and the bite of crunchy vegetables combine to make this relish a relevant condiment on urban tables too!

**1 quart chopped cabbage
2 cups chopped green tomatoes
2 cups chopped red tomatoes
1½ to 2 cups cauliflower florets
1 large green pepper, chopped
1 tablespoon dried hot pepper
 flakes
1 cup dark brown sugar, packed
1 cup chopped onions
1 clove garlic, finely chopped
Kernels from 1 ear of raw corn
1½ teaspoons ground ginger
¾ teaspoon ground cinnamon
¾ teaspoon ground cloves
1 tablespoon turmeric
¾ teaspoon curry powder
¾ teaspoon celery seed
1½ teaspoons kosher salt
1 tablespoon cornstarch
1 tablespoon English dry mustard
1 cup cider vinegar**

Combine all but the last 3 ingredients in a large saucepan.

Combine the cornstarch, mustard and vinegar in a small bowl; mix thoroughly. Pour the mixture over the vegetables. Bring to a boil over moderate heat. Simmer, stirring frequently, for about 1 hour. Pour into hot sterilized jars. Seal and store in a cool place.

Condiments & Spicy Sauces

Do not look a spicy gift horse in the mouth!" is an expression that always comes to the authors' minds, particularly the week before Christmas when gift lists proliferate as unexpectedly as house guests, and pickings at the local markets are not only slim but pricey. Barring a windfall inheritance (and a shopping spree at Tiffany's), homemade tangy condiments and sauces make great stocking stuffers. Every one of the following mayonnaises, mustards and savory sauces will add zip to the holidays and even beyond with any luck at all. More to the point, each is affordable and relatively simple to make, even in a tiny apartment kitchen. We know!

Some of the condiments and sauces come with a caveat, however. They are fairly fragile and hold up best under refrigeration. Any airtight jar or container will do nicely for giving—faceted jelly jars, thin olive jars, squat mustard jars—in fact, any unusual bottle. Make sure to tag each item with the date of shelf-life expiration, prominently displayed.

Caribbean Mustard

Makes 1 pint

All fine mustards are made from either black or white mustard seeds, very finely ground, then boiled and steeped in vinegar, sour must of wine, and a variety of regional seasonings to add flavor. Our favorite homemade mustard sauce depends on a splash of dark rum for its unusual savor.

Cellophane-wrapped smoked meats and chicken, or an array of unusual sausages, tucked into a basket with a jar of this mustard, make a welcome gift any day.

¼ cup English dry mustard
½ cup tarragon wine vinegar
1½ tablespoons dark rum
3 eggs
6 tablespoons granulated sugar
8 tablespoons unsalted butter
½ teaspoon salt
Pinch of freshly ground pepper

Place the mustard in a small bowl; add the vinegar and rum but do not stir. Cover and let stand overnight.

Place the mustard mixture in the top of a double boiler. Whisk over simmering water until smooth. Add the eggs, one at a time, beating thoroughly after each addition. Gradually stir in the sugar. Beat in the butter, 1 tablespoon at a time, and season with the salt and pepper. Cook, stirring constantly, until thick, about 5 minutes. Spoon into sterilized jars. Cool and seal. Store in the refrigerator. It will keep about 2 weeks.

Roasted Pepper Mayonnaise

Makes about 1 pint

One of the best homemade sauces to liven a broiled fillet of fish or a cold chicken leg—is a silken mayonnaise sauce that has been dappled with stripes of roasted green and red peppers for pungency. A wonderful gift to look at, it is even better to eat.

1 red pepper
1 green pepper
2 egg yolks
1 tablespoon wine vinegar
Juice of ½ lemon
½ teaspoon soy sauce
Pinch of ground white pepper
1½ teaspoons Dijon mustard
1 cup vegetable oil
½ cup olive oil
Dash of hot pepper sauce
1 shallot, finely chopped
1 tablespoon boiling water

Turn on the broiler or grill, or preheat the oven to 350 degrees.

Blanch the peppers in plenty of boiling water for 2 minutes. Drain thoroughly. Roast on a covered grill over direct heat until charred and soft, about 30 minutes, or bake on a foil-lined baking sheet in the preheated oven for 50 minutes. Cool.

Peel the peppers with a sharp knife. Chop them finely and set aside.

Beat the egg yolks in a large bowl until light. Slowly beat in the vinegar, lemon juice, soy sauce, white pepper and mustard. Beat in the oils, 1 tablespoon at a time, until the mayonnaise is thick. Add hot pepper sauce, the shallot, the tablespoon of boiling water and chopped peppers; mix well. Pour into sterilized jars. Seal and refrigerate for up to 5 days.

Homemade Pistachio Nut Oil

Makes about 1 half-pint

The next recipe is borrowed frankly from the culinary handicraft of talented author, and friend, Paula Wolfert. The authority on the foods of Morocco and Southwestern France, she makes a semiauthentic nutted oil out of vegetable oil steeped with walnuts. We substituted pistachio nuts on occasion and found their subtle flavor made an amazing and aromatic difference. The oil takes on a light green tint from the pistachios and should be packaged in clear glass bottles. Make a note on the tag to store it in a dark, cool place.

½ pound pistachio nuts, shelled
1⅓ cups vegetable oil

Place the shelled pistachios on a baking sheet and warm in a 300-degree oven for 5 minutes.

Transfer the nuts to a sheet of wax paper and crush them with a rolling pin. Place in a wide-mouthed glass quart jar. Pour the oil over the nuts. Do not stir. Seal and let stand in the refrigerator for 7 days.

Strain the oil twice through a fine sieve. Pour into attractive glass jars, cork and seal. Store in a cool place.

NOTE: This recipe may be doubled.

Vinaigrette Sauce

Makes about 3 half-pints

Vinegar was once used as a prophylactic to ward off the plague. Without being extravagant, we can claim that this will certainly forestall dietary doldrums for the recipient. It's the best friend a slaw ever had and in itself a tonic for cold cooked vegetables or shrimp. Give a half-pint or whole pint in a pretty glass or pottery decanter—and warn the beneficiary that the vinaigrette's shelf life is limited to 4 to 5 days in the refrigerator.

3 small cloves garlic, crushed
1½ teaspoons kosher salt
1 tablespoon Dijon mustard
Juice of 1½ lemons
1½ cups vegetable or olive oil
2 tablespoons red wine vinegar
1½ teaspoons freshly ground
** pepper**

Place the garlic and salt in a bowl and mash together with the back of a spoon until the mixture forms a paste.

Stir in the mustard and lemon juice. Whisk in the oil, vinegar and pepper. Pour into sterilized jars or bottles. Seal. Store in the refrigerator, briefly.

Homemade Tomato Sauce

Makes about 1½ pints

The following tomato sauce is a very satisfying embroidery for pasta, and always a welcome gift. The secret is the butter, so don't be skimpy. Make sure you note on the label that it must be kept refrigerated. The shelf life? About 2 weeks. Ground-glass apothecary bottles, sealed with red wax, make decidedly unusual gift containers.

8 ounces unsalted butter
8 large ripe tomatoes, peeled,
** seeded and chopped**
2 medium-size yellow onions,
** chopped**
2 cloves garlic, mashed
2 stalks celery, finely chopped
2 teaspoons chopped fresh basil
** or 1 teaspoon dried**
2 teaspoons chopped fresh
** oregano or 1 teaspoon dried**
1 teaspoon chopped fresh thyme
** or ⅛ teaspoon dried**
2 tablespoons granulated sugar
½ teaspoon grated orange peel

Heat the butter in a medium-sized saucepan over low heat. Add the remaining ingredients. Increase the heat to moderate and cook, stirring frequently, until thick. Pour into hot sterilized jars. Seal. Cool and refrigerate.

All-American Barbecue Sauce

Makes 1½ to 2 pints

If one had to choose a most "typical" American barbecue sauce, this would be it—right down to the obligatory ketchup, Worcestershire and A-1 Sauce. It's a good basic all-around sauce. P.S. A batch may be made up in a half-hour flat!

We pack this sauce into large ketchup bottles (adorned with gilt stars) for the barbecue lovers on our list.

2 tablespoons unsalted butter
2 medium-size onions, finely
   chopped
1½ cups ketchup
6 tablespoons brown sugar
6 tablespoons Worcestershire
   sauce
¼ cup prepared steak sauce
2 tablespoons cider vinegar
½ cup water
⅛ teaspoon hot pepper sauce

Heat the butter in a medium-sized saucepan over moderately low heat. Add the onions and sauté for 5 minutes, but do not allow them to brown. Stir in the remaining ingredients. Bring to a boil; reduce the heat and simmer, stirring occasionally, for 20 minutes. Pour into hot sterilized jars. Seal. Cool, and refrigerate for up to 2 weeks.

California Barbecue Sauce

Makes about 1½ pints

A sauce of a different color, this thick, golden apricot puree is similar to Chinese duck sauce, which is devised from pickled plums. An unusual combination of sweet and sour, it is a natural accompaniment for spareribs, and smoked or fresh ham. A note to that effect might be fastened to the jar, plus obligatory furbelows, of course.

⅔ cup dried apricots
3 cups water
2 shallots, finely chopped,
   or 2 scallions, finely chopped
1 cup tarragon vinegar
½ cup honey
½ cup ketchup
6 tablespoons vegetable oil
1 teaspoon soy sauce
1 teaspoon crumbled leaf oregano
1 teaspoon salt
½ teaspoon freshly ground
   pepper

Combine the apricots and water in a medium-sized saucepan. Bring to a boil over moderate heat and simmer until tender, about 25 minutes. Cool slightly.

Drain the apricots over a measuring cup. Place the apricots and 1 cup of the drained liquid (add water if necessary to make up 1 cup) in the container of a blender or food processor. Blend until smooth, being careful as hot liquid will splash upward.

Combine the apricot puree and all the remaining ingredients in a medium-sized saucepan and bring to a boil. Remove from the heat and pour into hot sterilized jars. Seal. Cool and refrigerate for up to 2 weeks.

Two Horseradish Sauces

There is nothing more satisfying for dieters than a sharp, low-calorie pick-me-up for unadorned broiled or grilled meat dishes. Consider packaging small jars of the following ruby red and bright green condiments for any weight watcher in your circle. Be warned that the green variety, in particular, is hot as the very dickens; do not press it on any lily-livered friends. Make both condiments in a processor for supreme ease and little kitchen time.

BEET RED HORSERADISH

Makes about 1 pint

4 large beets
1 medium-size fresh horseradish
  root
½ cup red wine vinegar
2 tablespoons honey

Cook the beets in boiling salted water until tender, about 15 minutes. Rinse under cold running water until cool; drain and peel.

Peel the horseradish and grate, using the grating blade of a food processor. You should have 2 cups. Grate the beets in the same manner.

Fit the processor with a steel blade and place the horseradish and beets in the container. Add the remaining ingredients. Process until finely chopped.

BITING GREEN HORSERADISH

Makes about 1 half-pint

1 medium-size fresh horseradish
  root
½ cup chopped fresh parsley
⅓ cup white wine vinegar
1 teaspoon sugar
2 to 3 tablespoons water
Salt to taste

Peel the horseradish and grate, using the grating blade of a food processor. You should have 2 cups.

Fit the processor with a steel blade and place the grated horseradish in the container. Add the remaining ingredients. Process until finely chopped. If the mixture seems too thick, add more water.

Pernod Tartar Sauce

Makes 3 half-pints

There are tartar sauces and tartar sauces but none has the mystical zest of this one. The delicate flavor of licorice makes it special; and it absolutely cannot be whipped up without a spoonful of anise-flavored Pernod. Give a jar to any fish lover of your acquaintance. If you want to be really extravagant, the sauce can be spooned into a crock (with cover) and accompanied by a smoked fish on a fish board. Wrap it securely in plastic wrap, before adding any ribbons or tags.

1 cup mayonnaise, preferably
  homemade
½ teaspoon Dijon mustard
2 tablespoons Pernod
2 teaspoons lemon juice
2 small shallots, finely
  chopped
2 teaspoons chopped fresh
  parsley
4 teaspoons chopped fresh dill
1 teaspoon chopped fresh chives
2 sour gherkins or cornichons,
  finely chopped
Salt and freshly ground pepper

Whisk the mayonnaise with the mustard, Pernod and lemon juice in a bowl until smooth. Add the shallots, parsley, dill, chives and gherkins; mix thoroughly. Add salt and pepper to taste. Pour into jars. Seal. Store in the refrigerator up to 7 days.

Spinach Pesto

Makes about 1 pint

This bright green sauce should probably be called "Presto" for it is exceedingly easy to make. The flavor of raw green spinach is intoxicatingly different, so press a jar on any true aficionado of Italian dishes—along with a sheaf of fresh (or frozen) pasta, tied with a red ribbon to echo the colors of the Italian flag.

1 pound fresh spinach
3 cloves garlic
½ cup walnut meats
½ cup olive oil
¼ cup freshly grated Parmesan
  cheese
½ teaspoon salt or to taste

Trim the stems from the spinach. Wash the leaves several times in cold water. Drain; pat dry with paper towels.

Combine the spinach, garlic, walnuts and oil in the container of a food processor or blender. Process until smooth. Stir in the cheese; mix thoroughly and add salt to taste. Spoon into a sterilized jar, seal, and store in the refrigerator for up to 2 weeks.

Pickles

A pickle is technically any food that has been preserved in a brine solution and flavored with herbs or spicy seasonings. In our mutual backgrounds, however, a pickle always meant some type of vegetable (most often a gherkin) that retained a healthy degree of crunch after its stint in the barrel. Bert Greene's mother used to refer to properly matured pickles as "molar material"—they had to be really firm to get her vote.

The best maker of molar materials in our circle of pickle-makers is Phillip Schulz's younger sister, Linda Herbert, of Morrison, Colorado. Her pickles always have the exactly correct degree of "bite" to meet our specification and the secret, or so Linda claims, is dill blossoms going to seed and pickling salt. So do not make substitutions for either ingredient and expect to duplicate her ultimate offering.

Linda Herbert's Dills

Makes about 6 pints

5 cups water
1 cup cider vinegar
½ cup pickling or kosher salt
20 to 25 small cucumbers
   (gherkins), rinsed
Fresh dill tops gone to seed
   or fresh dill sprigs with
   dried dill seeds

Combine water, vinegar and salt in a medium-sized saucepan and bring to a boil, stirring to dissolve the salt. Remove from the heat and let cool for 10 minutes.

Pack the cucumbers into sterilized 1-pint jars. Add to each jar either 1 dill top with seeds, or 1 fresh dill sprig with 2 teaspoons dried dill seeds. Pour the vinegar mixture into each jar to cover. Seal, and place in a hot-water bath for 10 minutes. Cool the jars upside down.

NOTE: Let the pickles stand at least 8 weeks before using. Serve well chilled. French canning jars (with wire closures) make very attractive pickle pots.

Dilled Carrots

Makes 1 pint

A pickle of a different stripe, these carrots are pickled overnight and then folded into green-specked sour cream. Shelf life (in the refrigerator) is about 3 days. For a longer lasting snack, keep the carrots in the pickling brine.

Pack in a recycled olive jar, tied up with a carrot-shaped pincushion to make the pickle's origin perfectly clear.

4 large carrots, cut into
   2-by-¼-inch strips
1½ cups dill pickle juice
1 cup sour cream
1½ tablespoons finely chopped
   chives
¼ cup chopped fresh dill
Salt and freshly ground pepper

Simmer the carrot strips in the pickle juice in a small saucepan over moderate heat until tender, about 15 minutes. Let the carrots cool in the juice. Chill them overnight, still in the juice.

Beat the sour cream in a large bowl until smooth. Add the chives and 3 tablespoons of the dill. Drain the carrots, and toss into the sour cream mixture. Season to taste with salt and pepper. Add remaining 1 tablespoon dill. Spoon into sterilized jars, seal, and refrigerate. For a more decorative gift, pack in a covered glass dish.

Fast 'n' Easy Refrigerator Pickles

Makes 3 pints

These pickles can be made anytime, anywhere. There is no cooking involved (other than sterilizing the jars). In three days' time, you will have a wonderful, no-fuss, crispy batch of pickles. Pack several jars of pickles into a drawstring shopping bag for a pickle-loving friend.

4 medium-size cucumbers, thinly sliced
2 medium-size onions, halved, thinly sliced
1 medium-size green pepper, thinly sliced
1 tablespoon salt
1 cup granulated sugar
1 cup red wine vinegar
¼ cup water
1 teaspoon celery seeds

Combine the cucumbers, onions and green pepper in a bowl. Sprinkle with salt; let stand 1 hour. Drain.

Combine the sugar, vinegar, water and celery seeds in a bowl. Stir until the sugar dissolves (do not heat).

Pack the cucumber mixture into sterilized jars. Add enough of the sugar-vinegar liquid to each jar to cover. Seal. Refrigerate the pickles at least 3 days before eating.

Store Bread and Butter Pickles

Makes about 3 pints

We used to make these in large quantities at The Store in Amagansett, and they were so popular we could barely keep them on the shelf. Wrap a jar of pickles in bright tissue with a pickle fork as a gift bonus.

1½ quarts medium-size cucumbers, sliced
2 medium-size onions, sliced
¼ cup kosher salt
Water, to cover the cucumbers
1 cup cider vinegar
¼ cup water
1¼ cups sugar
1 tablespoon mustard seed
½ teaspoon celery seed
½ teaspoon turmeric

Combine the cucumbers and onions in a large bowl. Add salt, toss well, and let stand 1 hour. Cover with cold water; let stand 2 hours longer. Drain well.

Combine the remaining ingredients in a large saucepan and bring to a boil. Add the cucumbers and onions, return to the boil, and simmer 10 minutes. Do not over-boil; the pickles should be crunchy.

Pack, immediately, into hot sterilized jars. Seal. Store in a cool dark place at least 4 weeks.

Sweet Zucchini Chips

Makes 1½ pints

As deep-dyed pickle lovers, we always look for one notable characteristic in every gherkin: adequate crunch. These green zucchini squash slices possess that quality in spades. They are also very easy to make but come with a mild warning: Do not overcook them!

Pack in a large jar, place in a basket of raw zucchini with the recipe attached. Plus a card reading: "REFILLS UP TO YOU!"

2 medium-size zucchini (about ¾ pound), thinly sliced
1 small yellow onion, halved, thinly sliced
1½ tablespoons salt
1 cup distilled white vinegar
½ cup sugar
½ teaspoon celery seeds
½ teaspoon anise seeds
1 teaspoon dry mustard

Place the zucchini and onion in a bowl. Sprinkle with salt; add cold water to cover and let stand for 1 hour.

Combine the remaining ingredients in a medium-sized heavy pot. Bring to a boil and remove from the heat.

Strain the zucchini and onions. Stir them into the vinegar mixture in the pot and let stand for 1 hour.

Bring the zucchini mixture to a boil and cook for 2 minutes. Pour into sterilized jars and seal. Place the jars in a hot-water bath for 10 minutes. Cool, and store in a cool place for at least 4 weeks.

Mediterranean Onion Pickle

Makes about 2 pints

These pickled onions are a gift from the South of France that Greene first tasted in Beaulieu. Telling tales of this wonderful, chutneylike pickle, we managed to reconstruct it at home. It's a winner—sure to please even deep-dyed pickle-phobes! These onion pickles may be packed into sterilized canning jars or interesting marmalade or mustard crocks. If using a crock, find a cork to fit the top and seal with wax for security.

1 cup dry white wine
½ cup white wine vinegar
2½ cups water
¾ cup currants
1 cup granulated sugar
⅓ cup olive oil
½ cup chopped tomatoes
3 small bay leaves, crumbled
3 sprigs fresh thyme, chopped,
  or ⅛ teaspoon dried
1 teaspoon salt
½ teaspoon freshly ground
  pepper
¼ teaspoon cayenne pepper
1 tablespoon unsalted butter
1 tablespoon vegetable or
  olive oil
2½ pounds tiny white onions,
  peeled, with a cross cut in each
  root end
6 ounces white button
  mushrooms

Place all but the last four ingredients in a large, heavy saucepan. Bring to a boil over moderate heat.

Meanwhile, heat the butter and 1 tablespoon oil in a heavy skillet. Brown the onions on all sides over high heat, shaking the pan frequently. Transfer the onions to the saucepan with a slotted spoon. Boil over high heat for 15 minutes, stirring frequently.

Reduce the heat and add the mushrooms. Simmer until the mushrooms are soft and the mixture has the texture of a slightly runny chutney, about 5 to 10 minutes. (Do not overcook, as the mixture will become too thick.) Pour into hot sterilized jars—or crocks, if you will be keeping no longer than 4 weeks. Seal and cool. Refrigerate.

Gifts in Jars

(Jams, Jellies, Fruit Butters, Marmalades, Conserves and Sweet Sauces)

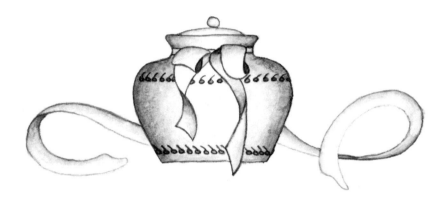

As stated earlier, most of our "cooking for giving" is done at the last minute out of necessity. The time for jam-or-jellying and marmalade-making gets squeezed into the calendar whenever there is an opening, not just in summer. And we advise you to profit by our example.

The authors learned out-of-season preservation the hard way. At least twice a summer, independently of each other, both of us found ourselves afflicted with a curious malady (inherited from maternal forebears, no doubt): the irresistible urge to fill our cupboards with homemades. But though we acquired glass Ball jars in really large numbers and stocked up on every reddening and ripening fruit on the vine, we had neither energy nor space to face the steamy business of putting them in jars, and rarely got around to it until they were well past their prime.

These days, with never more than three pint jars at the boil in the saucepan that makes do as a sterilizer, the stuff *does* get "put up." Precisely because it is no sweat for the cooks. And the tiny hallway closet that does double service as a cold cellar is stocked with a sufficiency of gleaming jars all year round.

Jams, Jellies, Fruit Butters

◉

G reene and Schulz have a hard-and-fast rule (no, make that a crotchet) about jam, jelly and fruit-butter making. We positively never use commercial pectin to thicken a spoonful. Why? Out of tradition; neither of our mothers or grandmothers used it. Also, it seems a textural disrespect to really ripe fruit.

Most of the jam and jelly recipes that follow will produce a slightly runny (though intensely flavorsome) *confiture* of fresh fruit, for we also do not believe in oversweetening or overcooking our homemades. Test for thickness, once a batch of jam or jelly has cooked, by placing a scant spoonful on a saucer that has had a short stint in the freezer. If the jam coagulates sufficiently for your palate, jar the batch at once. If you prefer a thicker consistency, allow the batch to cool completely. Then, after scraping down the sides of the pan carefully with a wooden spoon, bring the mixture back to the boil for an additional 10 to 15 minutes. But stir the reheated jam or jelly often because the sugar has a tendency to scorch.

Super Strawberry Jam
Makes about 4½ pints

Time was when Schulz's sister Linda Herbert would send the authors a batch of her very special homemade strawberry jam. However, since Linda has turned her attention to remarkable hand-crafted dolls and toys, we are forced to make our own. Everybody loves homemade strawberry jam. Hers, like ours, is slightly runny.

4 pints strawberries, washed and hulled (about 6 cups)
6 cups granulated sugar (approximately)

Cut any large strawberries in half. (You should have about 6 cups in all.) Place the strawberries in a large, heavy pot. Add the sugar to the berries (1 cup sugar for each 1 cup fruit). Bring quickly to the boil. Boil rapidly for 20 minutes. Cool slightly.

Pour the jam into sterilized jars; seal.

True Blue Blueberry Jam

Nothing turns a blueberry's mood indigo faster than a splash of citrus. Orange is the quintessential alliance, in our opinion. If you have a taste for blueberries, nothing can top this. Your friends and relatives will agree. At Christmas, we pack jars of jam (as trios or quartets of varied flavors) in contrasting shades of tissue papers and give them to beloved friends in small, brightly colored shopping bags.

2½ pints blueberries, picked over and washed
Finely slivered rind of 1 large orange
Pulp of 1 large orange, thinly sliced
5 cups granulated sugar
½ cup Orange Liqueur (page 84)

Combine blueberries, orange rind, orange pulp and sugar in a large, heavy saucepan. Bring to a boil. Simmer until the blueberries begin to pop and the jam thickens, from 10 to 15 minutes. Remove from the heat and stir in the orange liqueur. Pour into hot sterilized jars. Seal. Store in a cool place.

End-of-the-Blackberries Jam

Last fruits are reputed to be the sweetest. We usually buy blackberries for jam in late August so there will be a jar left in the cupboard to remind us of summer, on the coldest day ahead. Unfortunately, packaged frozen berries are not widely available in the Northeast, so preparation time is preordained. Whenever you make it, this orange-scented jam is the best friend a slice of toast will ever have!

2 pints fresh blackberries (about 4 cups)
¼ cup orange juice
1 teaspoon finely grated orange peel
4 cups sugar
¼ teaspoon ground cinnamon

Pick over the berries and wipe gently with a damp cloth.
Place the orange juice with the berries in a medium-sized heavy pot and bring to a boil. Add the orange peel, sugar, and cinnamon. Return to boiling and boil until the jam thickens on a chilled plate, about 20 minutes. Pour into sterilized jars and seal. Store in a cool place.

Pure Raspberry Jam

Makes about 2 pints

The most seductive perfume in the world (to both the authors) is not created by Chanel, Dior or St. Laurent. What makes our nostrils flare is much simpler stuff: the scent of a newly opened jar of ripe, red raspberry jam. For out-of-season putter uppers it might be worth noting that we have made this in early December (and late March, too) using frozen raspberries (drained of syrup), decreasing the initial portion of the cooking time to 20 minutes, then proceeding as directed.

2 cups raspberries, mashed
2 cups granulated sugar
Juice of ¼ lemon
Juice of ¼ orange

Cook the berries in a medium-sized saucepan over low heat, stirring often, for 30 minutes.

Add ½ cup of the sugar and slowly bring to a boil. Gradually add the lemon and orange juice, alternating with the remaining sugar, and bringing the syrup back to a boil after each addition.

When the jam has thickened, remove it from the heat and ladle it into hot sterilized jars. Seal. Store in a cool place.

Grape Jam

Makes 3 to 3½ pints

The best grape jam that either of us has ever made is a legacy from Bert Greene's grandmother. We have always felt it to be special, as has the lucky recipient of a spare jar here or there. But our feelings were confirmed when a dear friend, M.F.K. Fisher, recently gave us a jar of the very same jam. We relished every drop.

2 pounds Muscadine or
    Concord grapes
¾ cup water
2½-3 cups granulated sugar
½ stick cinnamon bark
⅛ teaspoon ground cloves
Rind of ¼ orange, finely grated
2 tablespoons Grand Marnier

Skin the grapes. (It is best to use rubber gloves for this.) Save the skins and the pulp in separate bowls.

Combine the grape pulp and water in a medium-sized saucepan and cook over moderately-high heat for 15 minutes. Put the cooked pulp through a fine sieve to remove the seeds. Save the pulp and juice; discard the seeds.

Return the pulp to the saucepan. Add the skins and the sugar. Cook slowly until slightly thickened, about 15 minutes. Add the cinnamon, cloves and grated orange rind.

Cook slowly until the jam is quite thick, about 15 minutes. Add the Grand Marnier and simmer for 5 minutes longer.

Remove the cinnamon stick. Pour the jam into hot sterilized jars. Seal. Store in a cool place.

Vanilla-Peach

Makes about 2 pints

The following recipe is a family treasure, passed on to us by Chris Fagon, a treasure herself, whom we met at a cooking school called The Pampered Pantry in Clayton, Missouri. A hint of vanilla endows the preserves with the most intoxicating flavor we have ever encountered in a jar. Gold should taste so good!

P.S. Chris's jam is on the runny side. Should you desire a thicker preserve, increase the second and third boiling periods by 10 minutes each. But test the jam for doneness before you pour it into jars.

2 pounds ripe peaches
2-inch piece vanilla bean
2 cups sugar
2 teaspoons lemon juice

Plunge the peaches into boiling water for about 30 seconds to loosen the skins. Drain. Cool and peel. Cut into slices.

Place the peach slices in a heavy pot, bring to a boil, and boil for 10 minutes. Strain into another heavy pot. Reserve the slices.

Bring the peach juice to a boil. Add the vanilla bean, lemon juice and sugar. Return to boiling and boil for 20 minutes.

Split the vanilla bean and scrape the seeds into the peach liquid. Return the peach slices to the liquid also, and boil until the jam thickens on a chilled plate, about 10 minutes. Pour into sterilized jars and seal. Place in a hot-water bath for 10 minutes. Store in a cool place.

Melon Jam

Makes 3 pints

Honeydew is usually part of our "after-summer" jam sessions. Dubbed a winter melon, this fruit actually appears in early fall, but stores so well that it is generally available long after the Christmas season.

1 large, or 2 small, honeydew
**   melons (about 5 pounds)**
½ teaspoon lime peel
Pulp and juice of 2 limes
4½ cups sugar
Juice of 1 lemon

Cut the melon in half and remove the seeds. Using a sharp spoon or melon cutter, scrape out the pulp. You should have about 4 cups. Place in a large, heavy pot. Add the lime peel, pulp and lime juice. Bring to a boil and add the sugar. Return to boiling and boil until the jam thickens on a chilled plate, about 45 minutes.

Add the lemon juice to the melon jam. Pour into sterilized jars and seal. Store in a cool place.

Quick-and-Easy Mint Jelly

Makes about 1½ pints

A trick we learned a long time ago, and a wonderful tip for a quick gift when you know you will be offered lamb for dinner. Fill an antique covered sugar bowl or jam jar with this "fake" mint jelly. Secure the top with tape, then wrap generously in cellophane.

10-ounce jar mint apple jelly
¼ cup green crème de menthe
1 cup chopped fresh mint leaves
1 tablespoon wine vinegar
Dash of freshly ground pepper

Combine all the ingredients in a bowl. Stir until smooth. Pour into a gift container or a sterilized jar. Seal. Store in the refrigerator.

Peach Butter

Makes about 2½ pints

Peaches and cinnamon are born flavor mates. Come late August we are knee-deep in peach pits, skimming the sweet aromatic fuzz from a gallon pot of yellow gold.

3¼ pounds peaches
¼ of a large orange
1½ cups granulated sugar
  (approximately)
½ cinnamon stick
Dash of almond extract

Drop the peaches into boiling water for several minutes to loosen the skins. Remove the skins and reserve them. Discard the pits and cut the peaches into ½-inch slices. Place in a colander over a bowl and let stand for 20 minutes to collect the juice.

Remove the rind from the orange section and add to the reserved peach skins. Seed the orange and chop the pulp. Place the peach skins and orange pulp in a large, heavy pot and add juice. Cook over low heat until the peach skins are tender, about 15 minutes. Place in a blender container, and blend until smooth.

Return the peach-skin puree to the pot. Add the sliced peaches, sugar and cinnamon stick. Boil 30 minutes. Skim the froth from the top of the liquid as it boils.

Remove the cinnamon stick. Place the peach mixture in a blender container, 2 cups at a time; puree until smooth, being careful as hot liquids splash upward. Stir in the almond extract and return the peach mixture to pot. Bring to a boil; remove from the heat.

Taste for sweetness and stir in additional sugar, if desired. Place in a hot-water bath for 20 minutes. Store in a cool place.

Marmalade

◉

What turns a batch of oranges and sugar (or any other fruit for that matter) into *marmalade* and not jelly is no question of semantics but rather hard-and-fast peel. The inclusion of the skin of the fruit (which also contains natural pectin for thickening) is what makes a marmalade marvelous.

The peel of fruit protects the fruit it surrounds, but in citrus fruits particularly, it also contains essential oils that intensify and deepen the fruit's natural flavor. However, the oil can be bitter, and the skin downright unpleasant-tasting if the white underskin enters the marmalade pot. It is imperative that the prime layer of skin be carefully peeled away with a rotary peeler in order to remove none of the bitter under layer. If there is a coating of white on the underside of any shorn peel, scrape it off carefully with a sharp knife. A short (two- to three-minute) blanching period in boiling water plus a douse in ice water will eliminate most bitterness.

Rhubarb-Cherry Marmalade
Makes 3 pints

In our book, marmalade is always a marriage of two disparate fruits united by orange peel. The blending of rhubarb and cherry is an alliance you will not soon forget, for it is a proven palate pleaser. Both ingredients may be selected in frozen form for a winter session at the jam pots. But make certain all fruit defrosts (and is drained) before you proceed with the marmalade-making.

1½ pounds fresh rhubarb,
  trimmed, cut into ½-inch pieces
2 cups plus ½ cup
  granulated sugar
⅔ cup orange juice
Flesh of ¼ orange, chopped
Finely slivered rind of ¼ orange
1 pound fresh cherries, pitted
¼ cinnamon stick
1 clove
1 tablespoon Orange Liqueur
  (page 84)

Combine the rhubarb, 2 cups of the sugar, ½ cup orange juice, and the orange flesh and rind in a large saucepan. Bring slowly to a boil and cook until the rhubarb is very tender.

Combine the cherries, ½ cup sugar, the remaining orange juice, and the cinnamon and clove tied in cheesecloth in another saucepan. Bring to a boil; simmer until the cherries are tender but still have a slight "bite" to them, about 12 to 15 minutes. Remove from the heat. Remove the spices in cheesecloth.

Strain the rhubarb mixture, reserving the liquid. Boil the liquid until reduced by half, about 10 minutes. Return the rhubarb to the liquid, add the cherry mixture, and mix thoroughly. Stir in the orange liqueur. Pour into hot sterilized jars. Seal. Store in a cool place or in the refrigerator.

Clementine and Orange Marmalade

Makes about 3 pints

Clementines are intensely flavored, imported tangerines that appear on better greengrocers' counters about a month before Christmas—so in our kitchen they always end up as marmalade as a matter of course. Regular tangerines make do as an admirable standby, however.

10-12 clementines or
   8 tangerines
6 oranges
1 lemon, peeled and thinly sliced
1 cup orange juice
5 cups sugar
¼ cup Grand Marnier

Carefully peel the outer skins from the clementines and oranges. Place the peels in a small saucepan, cover with water and bring to a boil. Boil for 10 minutes; drain. Cover the peels with fresh water. Bring to a boil again and boil until tender, about 10 more minutes; drain. Allow the peels to cool, then cut them into slivers. Set aside.

Remove any white strands from the clementines and oranges; cut the flesh into thin slices. Combine with the lemon slices and orange juice in a medium-sized saucepan. Add enough water to cover, and bring to a boil. Add the sugar and simmer for 20 minutes. Add the slivered peels and Grand Marnier; simmer over low heat for 10 minutes more. Pour into hot sterilized jars. Seal. Store in a cool place or in the refrigerator.

Pineapple-Apricot Marmalade

Makes about 3 pints

A traditional British recipe, perfect for giving in conjunction with the Scones on page 62. Paired with a pretty jam server, it makes a very special gift for its eventual home.

1 large pineapple, peeled,
   cored and cubed (about 3 cups)
Flesh of 1 orange, chopped
½ cup orange juice
¼ cup lemon juice
1 tablespoon grated orange rind
1 teaspoon grated lemon rind
3 cups granulated sugar
11-ounce package dried apricots,
   cut into strips
Pinch of ground cloves
Pinch of ground cinnamon
¼ cup Orange Liqueur (page 84)
1½ cups roughly chopped walnuts

Place 2 cups of the pineapple cubes in the container of a food processor or blender. Blend until smooth. Combine the pureed pineapple with the remaining cubed pineapple in a large saucepan. Add the orange flesh, orange juice, lemon juice, grated rind and sugar. Bring to a boil; reduce the heat, stir in the apricots, and simmer until fairly thick, about 30 minutes. Add the cloves and cinnamon, stir in the orange liqueur and walnuts, and cook for 6 minutes longer. Pour into hot sterilized jars. Seal. Store in a cool place or in the refrigerator.

Haitian Carrot and Nut Marmalade

Makes about 2 pints

This is a somewhat exotic concoction that we picked up on assignment in Haiti at a time when few Americans were visiting that enigmatic island. Much to our pleasure it was a big hit this past Christmas. The Haitians use a local nut-flavored liqueur to give this marmalade its unusual tang; the Walnut Liqueur on page 84 is an ideal substitute.

**1 pound carrots, finely
   shredded**
Juice of 2 lemons
**Rind of 2 lemons, slivered
   (about 1½ tablespoons)**
½ cup orange juice
1½ cups granulated sugar
**Generous ½ teaspoon ground
   cinnamon**
Pinch of ground cloves
¼ cup walnut meats
¼ cup sliced almonds
¼ cup hazelnut or walnut liqueur

Combine the carrots, lemon juice, lemon rind, orange juice and sugar in a saucepan; let stand for 30 minutes.

Bring the mixture to a boil and cook until the carrots become translucent and syrup is quite thick, about 15 minutes. Add the cinnamon, cloves, walnuts and almonds and cook for 15 minutes longer, or until a small amount of the mixture firms up when placed on a saucer straight from the freezer.

Add the liqueur and mix thoroughly. Pour into hot sterilized jars. Seal. Store in a cool place or in the refrigerator.

Conserves

◉

A conserve (as opposed to a mere preserve) is always a mixture of fruit flavors, blended together in the jam pot for a highly original, sometimes astringent piquancy. Conserves are traditionally served to offset roasted meats in rather the same manner in which a savory follows a sweet at formal functions—to awaken the drowsy taste buds.

A conserve, in our opinion, makes a wonderful adjunct whenever a meal lacks character. Try a spoonful or two with cold roast lamb, veal or chicken, when only a spartan salad, bread and cheese comprise a light meal. Conserves turn leftovers into conspicuous consumption.

Blue-Blue Plum Conserve
Makes about 3 pints

What makes a blue plum bluer and truer? The answer is blueberries. This darkly blue conserve is the tastiest addition a slice of ham (or a fresh grapefruit half) could hope for, because it adds remarkable depth to those totally unalike flavors. Give it, bowed and banded, in a basket with freshly baked Oven Scones (see page 62), wrapped in a napkin (blue, of course).

1¼ pounds blue plums, pitted
  and halved
¼ teaspoon almond extract
2 cups blueberries, washed
  and hulled
1½ cups granulated sugar
1 cup brown sugar, packed
¼ teaspoon ground cinnamon
⅛ teaspoon ground ginger
¼ cup water
¼ cup orange juice
2 tablespoons Cognac

Sprinkle the plums with almond extract and let stand for 30 minutes.

Combine the plums, blueberries, both sugars, spices, water and orange juice in a medium-sized saucepan. Quickly bring to a boil; reduce the heat and simmer, stirring frequently, until the mixture is fairly thick, for about 1 hour.

Add the Cognac and simmer 10 to 15 minutes more. Pour into hot sterilized jars. Seal. Store in the refrigerator.

Cranberries in Grand Marnier

Makes about 2½ to 3 pints

The following cranberry conserve is one which your friends and relatives will give thanks for at any time of year. It is a far cry from the stuff that comes in a can—and it is truly one of the most asked-for items on our list of yearly "put ups."

To make your gift even more memorable cram these berries into an antique cranberry-glass container. Embellish with cellophane and ribbons at your own discretion.

1 pound cranberries
(about 4 cups)
1 cup orange juice
2 cups granulated sugar
Flesh of 1 orange, all pithy
parts removed, seeded
and chopped
2 tablespoons finely slivered
orange rind
½ cup Grand Marnier

Pick over cranberries and wash in a colander under cold running water.

Place the orange juice and sugar in a large saucepan; cook and stir over moderate heat until the sugar dissolves.

Add the cranberries, orange flesh and orange rind. Bring to a boil; then reduce the heat and simmer until the skins pop and cranberries are tender, 10 to 15 minutes. Add the Grand Marnier and simmer for 2 minutes longer. Pour into hot sterilized jars. Seal. Store in the refrigerator.

Cranberries in Red Wine

Makes about 1½ pints

Another cranberry favorite is French in origin and one Bert Greene picked up when he spent six months in Eze. It is a winter winner. Pack a generous hamper with cellophane and add a jar of these berries, plus a loaf of bread, a pack of chestnuts and a crock of Devilled Ham (page 20). They're highly compatible tastes served before a crackling fire.

12-ounce package fresh
cranberries
1½ cups granulated sugar
1 cup dry, full-bodied red wine
such as Cabernet Sauvignon
or Zinfandel
1 cinnamon stick (about 3 inches
long)
1 piece orange rind (about
7 inches long)

Pick over the cranberries, removing stems and any shriveled berries. Rinse under cold running water; drain.

Combine sugar and wine in a noncorrosive heavy medium-sized saucepan; bring to a boil, stirring constantly, over moderate heat. Stir in the cranberries, cinnamon stick and orange rind. Increase the heat to high and return the mixture to the boil, stirring constantly. Reduce the heat to medium-low; simmer, partially covered, stirring occasionally until the cranberries burst, 10 to 15 minutes.

Remove from the heat and discard the cinnamon stick. Lift out the piece of orange rind; let cool slightly. Cut it into thin julienne, then stir back into the cranberry mixture. Let cool to room temperature. Spoon into sterilized jars. Seal. Store in the refrigerator for up to 2 months.

Tomato-Plum Conserve

Revisit the soft radiance of harvest. Treasure it at your leisure in every bite of the following rosy conserve (dappled with plums, rippled with circles of cherry tomatoes). We like this conserve spread with a little cream cheese on a slice of homemade bread, but choose your own manner of comforting food to accompany it.

**3 pounds plums, pitted and
   roughly chopped
⅔ cup white wine
6 cups granulated sugar
Rind of ½ orange in one curl
½ large orange, thinly sliced
½ cup orange juice
Rind of ½ lemon, slivered
½ cinnamon stick
2 cups cherry tomatoes, halved**

Combine all the ingredients except the tomatoes, in a large saucepan. Bring to a boil over high heat and cook until slightly thickened, about 20 minutes. Remove the orange peel. Add the tomatoes, return to the boil, and cook for 20 minutes.

Pour into hot sterilized jars. Seal. Place in a hot-water bath for 10 minutes. Store in a cool place or in the refrigerator.

Apple Sorcery

Makes 3 pints

Phillip Stephen Schulz is the sorcerer here. He invented the following confection one fall afternoon when he had an excess of apples, practically no sugar, and a tangerine and pear in residence (in the refrigerator). His silky sauce/jam/conserve is thickened unpredictably with a jar of apricot preserves. The taste is terrific!

**6 Granny Smith apples, peeled,
    cored and sliced
Pulp of 1 orange
Pulp of 1 tangerine
1 large pear, peeled, cored
    and sliced
½ cup granulated sugar
¼ teaspoon ground cinnamon
12-ounce jar apricot preserves
½ teaspoon vanilla extract**

Combine all the ingredients except the vanilla in a large saucepan. Slowly bring to a boil; then reduce the heat and simmer until the fruit is soft, about 20 minutes.

Mash the fruit. Simmer until thickened, about 15 minutes. Stir in the vanilla. Pour into hot sterilized jars. Seal. Store in a cool place.

Quince and Almond Conserve

Makes about 3 pints

Speak of gleaming jars. Consider the glow of quince and the bite of almond as assets to bridge the seasons and provide double satisfaction—once to the maker in the preserving and later to the recipient in the eating.

**½ pound slivered almonds
5 pounds quinces, peeled, cored
    and cut into small pieces
Rind of 2 lemons, tied in
    cheesecloth
Juice of 2 lemons
6 cups granulated sugar
Rind of 2 oranges, cut into slivers**

Preheat the oven to 300 degrees.

Spread the almonds evenly in shallow baking pans. Place in the oven until delicately browned, 10 to 12 minutes. Set aside.

Place the quinces and lemon rinds in a medium-sized saucepan. Cover with water. Bring to a boil; reduce the heat and simmer until the fruit is soft, about 1 hour. Drain; reserve the liquid. Mash the quinces roughly until they are the texture of mashed turnips. Set aside.

Combine the reserved quince liquid and the lemon juice in the saucepan. Bring to a boil; simmer until the liquid is reduced to about 4 cups. Add the mashed quinces and orange slivers. Simmer for 15 minutes more. Remove from the heat and stir in the almonds. Pour into hot sterilized jars. Seal. Store in a cool place or in the refrigerator.

Blueberry Syrup

Makes about 2 pints

This favorite American pancake and waffle syrup comes from Better Than Store-Bought *(Harper & Row, 1979), a book no kitchen should be without, written by two good friends of ours, Helen Witty and Elizabeth Schneider Colchie. If you plan to give the syrup to your favorite pancake lover shortly after making it, the water bath can be skipped, but the syrup* must *then be stored in the refrigerator. Treat the recipient to this sauce poured into a cordial decanter—or an interestingly shaped, securely corked wine bottle.*

4 cups blueberries, stemmed and washed
3 cups water
2 curls lemon rind, about ½ inch wide by 3 inches long
3 cups sugar
Lemon juice to taste

Place the blueberries in a saucepan and mash well with a potato masher. Add 1 cup water and the lemon curls. Bring to a boil and simmer for 5 minutes. Strain through a fine sieve, pressing the berries with the back of a spoon. You should have about 2 cups of liquid.

Combine the remaining water with the sugar in a saucepan. Bring to a boil and boil until the mixture reaches 260 degrees on a candy thermometer. Add the blueberry liquid, and boil 1 minute more. Cool. Stir in lemon juice to taste. Pour into sterilized jars. Place in a hot-water bath for 30 minutes. Store in a cool place or in the refrigerator.

"Drop-Dead" Chocolate Sauce

Makes about 1 pint

On every cook's shelf of emergency rations, we ordain that there be at least one jar of a fabulous, fudgy sauce. No topping gives ice cream more clout nor converts store-bought pound cake into patisserie faster! The following sauce is dubbed "Drop-Dead" because it's quick to make and hard to resist. Store the jar in the refrigerator and warm it in a pan of hot, not boiling, water until runny, about 10 to 12 minutes.

½ **pound semisweet chocolate**
5 **tablespoons unsalted butter,**
   cut into small pieces
¼ **cup milk at room temperature**
¼ **cup heavy cream at room**
   temperature
2 **tablespoons dark rum**

Melt the chocolate in the top of a double boiler over hot water. Stir in the butter, bit by bit. Stir in the milk, cream and rum. Stir until very smooth. Pour the sauce into a sterilized jar. Cool and seal. Store in the refrigerator. Keeps 3 to 4 weeks.

Butterscotch Velvet Sauce

Makes 3½ pints

This is a rich and unctuous top coat that will do any fashionable ice cream sundae, frappé or banana split proud. Very thick and the color of gold ore, it is a lot less extravagant to prepare. We always make a double batch; one for giving and one for gorging. This topping should also be stored in the refrigerator—and warmed in a pan of hot, not boiling, water until somewhat runny, for about 10 to 12 minutes.

Pack a half-pint of this sauce along with the aforegoing "Drop-Dead" Chocolate Sauce plus a bunch of bananas and your favorite recipe for a banana split.

1¼ **cups brown sugar, packed**
4 **tablespoons strong, hot coffee**
4 **tablespoons unsalted butter**
14-**ounce can condensed milk**
4 **tablespoons heavy cream**

Combine the sugar, coffee and butter in a heavy saucepan. Cook over moderate heat until the sugar dissolves, about 3 to 5 minutes. Add the condensed milk. Cook, stirring constantly, for 5 minutes longer. Reduce the heat. Add the cream, cook for 2 minutes, then remove from the heat and allow to cool. Pour into sterilized jars, seal and refrigerate.

To reheat: Place the jar in warm water for 5 to 10 minutes. Stir thoroughly before pouring.

Nesselrode Sauce

Makes about 1 pint

Count Nesselrode was reputedly the inventor of one of the world's great sauces. However, his original recipe has passed through lots and lots of hands (including the authors') since it first saw light. Each has left some culinary stamp on the sauce—ours is the use of Amaretto liqueur. That touch of spirit makes this an imperative blanket for ice creams, custards and fruit compotes.

¼ **cup granulated sugar**
¼ **cup corn syrup**
½ **cup water**
⅔ **cup Amaretto (almond liqueur)**
½ **cup candied fruits**
¼ **cup chopped glazed cherries**
¼ **cup chopped glazed pineapple**
¼ **cup raisins**
¼ **cup chopped walnut meats**

Combine the sugar, corn syrup and water in a small saucepan. Bring to a boil and simmer, uncovered, for 5 minutes. Add the remaining ingredients; mix thoroughly. Spoon into sterilized jars. Seal. Refrigerate for several days before using.

NOTE: Nesselrode Sauce can be kept refrigerated for several weeks. The flavors develop on standing.

Classic Vanilla Sauce

Makes 1½ to 2 pints

This is a last-minute gift for last-minute giftees. It is perishable, however, and should be served within two or three days—a fact the donor should note on the label. We adapted this sauce from an Alice B. Toklas original and it has rated an unqualified WOW! from all recipients of our acquaintance. Add a splash to a simple dish (such as peeled, sliced oranges) or a complex one (such as Gâteau St. Honoré). Better yet, match a spoonful as topping to the Angel Cake on page 65.

6 egg yolks
1 cup granulated sugar
2¼ cups milk, scalded
1 teaspoon vanilla extract
1 tablespoon kirsch liqueur
½ **cup whipping cream, whipped until firm**

Beat the egg yolks with the sugar in the top of a double boiler. Whisk in the milk. Cook over hot water, stirring constantly, until thick, about 30 minutes. Remove from the heat.

Stir in the vanilla. Cool to room temperature.

Stir the kirsch into the sauce. Fold in the whipped cream. Pour into sterilized jars. Seal. Refrigerate until well chilled.

This sauce will keep for up to 2 days, stored in a very cold refrigerator.

Breads

If, at first glance, bread seems an odd choice for a cooked gift, please disabuse yourself of that notion. Breads (scones, biscuits or muffins) are literally "gifts from the hearth." They make handsome bestowals straight from the baker's rack or frozen rock-hard for a future defrosting. All such gifts should be wrapped in several layers of airtight plastic and foil before the decorative papers and ribbons are added. A nice touch (for an extravagant offering) is to place the bread in a bread basket or on a wooden board before surrounding it with cellophane. We always believe in clearly labeling the nature of the bread on a tag—and for safety's sake, noting the loaf's potential shelf life in the refrigerator or freezer.

Charles's Bread

Makes 2 loaves

We obtained the following recipe from a dashing lawyer of our acquaintance. Charles Sherman lives on Long Island and is obviously interested in healthful foods. This bread will be well received by anyone, as it is not only wholesome, but remarkably tasty.

Butter to grease baking pans
2 tablespoons dry yeast
2 cups warm water
3 tablespoons blackstrap molasses
5 tablespoons honey
5⅓ cups stone-ground whole-wheat flour (available in health food stores)
1½ teaspoons salt
3 tablespoons unsalted butter, softened
1 egg white, lightly beaten
⅔ cup sesame seeds (approximately)
2 tablespoons unsalted butter, melted

Butter 2 3-by-5-by-10-inch bread pans. Set aside.

Dissolve the yeast in warm water in a large bowl. Add the molasses and honey. Let stand for 10 minutes.

Stir in 3 cups of the whole-wheat flour. Add the salt and 3 tablespoons softened butter. Beat with a wooden spoon until smooth. Slowly add more flour, ½ cup at a time, until a stiff dough is formed. Turn onto a floured board; knead for 10 minutes.

Place the dough in a large, greased bowl. Cover and let rise in a warm place until doubled in bulk, about 1½ hours.

Punch down the dough. Knead for 5 minutes, then return to the bowl. Cover and let rise until again doubled in bulk, about 1 hour.

Punch down the dough and knead for 5 minutes. Divide the dough in half. Roll each half lengthwise into sausage shapes, each about 10 inches long. Beat each "sausage" flat with your hands, then fold the dough into thirds. Brush each loaf with egg white; roll in sesame seeds to coat completely. Place in the prepared bread pans. Cover with greased plastic wrap; let rise in a warm place for 50 minutes.

Heat the oven to 350 degrees. Bake the bread on a rack in the upper third of the oven until loaves sound hollow when tapped, about 45 minutes. Turn out on a wire rack. Brush the tops with melted butter to give the bread sheen.

Apple Butter and Honey Whole-Wheat Bread

Makes 2 medium-sized loaves

To ensure a splendidly crusty loaf, this bread should be sprayed with a mist of cold water the moment it goes into the oven and sprayed again after three minutes of baking. This recipe produces an unusual, delicately fruity flavor. We use homemade apple butter but store-bought does just fine, too. If you have an extra jar of homemade on hand, you might include it in the gift to underscore the originality of the loaf.

2 packages dry yeast
1 tablespoon granulated sugar
2 cups warm water
4 tablespoons unsalted butter,
  melted
½ cup apple butter
2 tablespoons honey
1½ tablespoons salt
3½ cups whole-wheat flour
2-2½ cups all-purpose flour
Cornmeal, for sprinkling
Egg wash: 1 egg beaten with
  1 teaspoon water

Dissolve the yeast and sugar in ½ cup warm water in a large bowl; let stand for 10 minutes. Stir in the remaining water, the butter, apple butter, honey and salt. Beat in the flour, 1 cup at a time. Turn out onto a floured board; knead until smooth, about 10 minutes. Shape into a ball and place in a well-buttered bowl; turn the dough to coat with butter. Cover with plastic wrap; let rise in a warm place until doubled in volume, about 1½ hours.

Punch down the dough; knead briefly. Shape the dough into 2 loaves. Cover, and let rise for 1 hour. (If you are using a baking sheet, sprinkle it with cornmeal and let the dough rise on the sheet.)

Preheat the oven to 425 degrees.

If you are using a tile baking surface, sprinkle it with cornmeal; transfer the bread loaves to the surface. Brush them with egg wash. Bake on a rack in the upper third of the preheated oven for 10 minutes; reduce oven heat to 375 degrees and bake 20 to 25 minutes longer, until the loaves sound hollow when tapped.

Oven Scones

Traveling in Great Britain a few years ago, we discovered the joys of "Cream Teas," which always mean a stopover for a pot of strong tea accompanied by a plate of freshly made scones, Devonshire cream, and homemade berry jam. Give your favorite friend a tin of these scones plus a jar of jam, and the following recipe for Mock Devonshire Cream. It's not authentic, but it's awfully good.

2 cups all-purpose flour
½ teaspoon baking soda
½ teaspoon cream of tartar
½ teaspoon salt
2 tablespoons unsalted butter, chilled
¾ to 1 cup buttermilk
Cornmeal

Preheat the oven to 475 degrees.

Sift the flour with the baking soda, cream of tartar and salt into a large bowl. Add the butter and blend with a pastry blender until well incorporated. Stir in the buttermilk, using a wooden spoon, starting with ¾ cup, and using just enough to form a soft dough.

Turn the dough out on a well-floured pastry board and sprinkle it lightly with flour. Knead for 2 minutes. Divide the dough in half. Shape each half into a ball. Roll each ball out ½ inch thick. Cut each into 4 pie-shaped wedges.

Sprinkle a baking sheet with cornmeal. Place the scones on the sheet about 1 inch apart. Bake on a rack in the upper third of the preheated oven until golden brown, about 15 to 20 minutes.

Mock Devonshire Cream

½ pint heavy cream
1 teaspoon confectioners' sugar
2 tablespoons sour cream

Beat the cream with confectioners' sugar until stiff. Slowly beat in the sour cream until the mixture becomes dense. Store in a covered jar in the refrigerator. Keeps about 2 to 3 days.

Old-Fashioned Cinnamon Ring

Serves 8

The original formula for a ring that Greene's grandmother used to make—glistening with cinnamon, melted sugar, and bits of almonds and pecans—has been lost to the ages. But this version comes very close indeed.

Wrap this loaf loosely with plastic wrap, so the wrap does not stick to the glaze, then house it in a tin, or a cake box worthy of its splended appearance. Tie a cinnamon stick in the ribbons to add an additional flavor note.

1 package dry yeast
Pinch of granulated sugar
¼ cup warm water
1 cup warm milk
8 tablespoons unsalted butter, melted
1¼ cups granulated sugar
1 teaspoon salt
3½-4 cups all-purpose flour
½ cup ground almonds
½ cup coarsely chopped pecans
¼ cup cookie crumbs
⅓ cup dried currants, soaked in Cognac for 1 hour
Ground cinnamon, to taste
Cornmeal, for sprinkling
1 egg, lightly beaten

ICING:
1 cup confectioners' sugar
2 tablespoons water
1 teaspoon rye whiskey

Dissolve the yeast with the pinch of sugar in warm water in a large bowl; let stand for 10 minutes. Stir in the milk, half the melted butter, ¼ cup sugar, the salt and 3 cups of the flour. Turn onto a lightly floured board. Knead, incorporating flour as required, until smooth and elastic, about 10 minutes. Shape into a ball; place in a lightly floured bowl. Cover tightly with plastic wrap; let rise in a warm place until doubled in volume, about 2 hours.

Punch down the dough and scrape it onto a lightly floured board. Let rest 3 minutes. Roll out to a 12-by-18-inch rectangle. Spread the remaining melted butter evenly over the surface. Combine 1 cup sugar with the almonds, pecans and cookie crumbs; spread the mixture evenly over the butter. Drain the currants; sprinkle over the entire surface. Sprinkle with cinnamon to taste. (We prefer a lot of cinnamon, but not everyone does.) Beginning with a long edge, roll up the dough.

Sprinkle a baking sheet with cornmeal; place the dough on the sheet, seam side down. Join the ends to form a ring; pinch the ends together to seal. Using a sharp knife, slice two-thirds of the way into the ring at 1½-inch intervals. Using 2 knives, gently press the top of each slice into a ridge, allowing the interior surfaces of slices to show. Cover with a flour-rubbed towel; let rise 1 hour.

Heat the oven to 350 degrees.

Brush the entire surface of ring with beaten egg. Bake until brown, 30 to 35 minutes.

Meanwhile, make the icing by whisking together the confectioners' sugar, water and rye whiskey until smooth. Spoon the icing over the warm cinnamon ring.

Cakes & Cookies

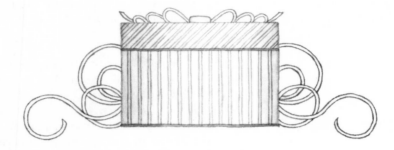

The fact that each of the authors has a sweet tooth of absolutely epic proportions makes the giving of cakes and cookies an especially noble gesture, because one of us always wants a sample slice and neither can claim self-control as his long suit.

Giving the gift of a cake requires a solid, airtight container. Round tin candy boxes make fine gift boxes for cookies and such, particularly if they are sprayed (with acrylic nontoxic paint only) and allowed to dry thoroughly before they are filled. Less intrepid bakers, however, may get by with any solid cardboard box that a cake or cookies will fit into compactly.

It is imperative to place any cake on a substantial round before it is sent on the road. You can purchase these at a baking supply house or make them at home by placing a sheet of heavy cardboard under the cake pan and tracing the circumference with a pencil. Cut out the inscribed circle with scissors and cover it with foil and a decorative doily. Do make sure to adhere a small piece of double-edged tape to the bottom of the round once the cake is in position, so the round does not slide about in the box. Send cake or cookie tins in larger, well-sealed, corrugated boxes surrounded with shredded paper or styrofoam "peanuts" as safeguards in transit.

Before the holidays, we tend to collect tins that other cakes and cookies came in and recycle them, daubed with stencilled patterns or studded with self-stick hearts, stars, or snowflakes that we find at party stores or fancy stationery departments. We have a good friend (with fine handwriting) who inevitably scrawls "This is a wonderful cake!" in gold indelible marker on brightly sprayed tins of every hue at Christmastime, and no one ever seems to argue with her dictum.

Chocolate Angel Cake

This dusky inspiration is for chocolate lovers everywhere; it is light, delicate, yet intensely cocoa-flavored. What makes the best chocolate angel cake is the best chocolate. We use Droste's cocoa. Give this dark angel in a wrap of plastic, then a box or bouquet of paper frills.

1¼ cups egg whites (about 10 to 12), at room temperature
1 teaspoon cream of tartar
1¼ cups granulated sugar
¼ teaspoon salt
¾ cup cake flour
¼ cup cocoa
1 teaspoon vanilla extract

Preheat the oven to 325 degrees.

Beat the egg whites until foamy; add the cream of tartar and beat until stiff but not dry.

Sift the sugar and salt together; beat gradually into the egg whites, about 2 tablespoons at a time. Add the vanilla. Combine the flour and cocoa; sift slowly into the meringue, ¼ cup at a time. Fold thoroughly after each addition.

Pour into an ungreased 10-inch tube pan. Bake in the preheated oven until a toothpick inserted in the center comes out clean, about 1 hour. Invert the pan on a rack and allow the cake to cool in the pan. Unmold.

Polka-Dot Angel Cake

This is a recent Greene/Schulz kitchen invention. We got the idea for this unique white-and-black confection just when the world deemed the chocolate chip craze had peaked. Now it may start again with fresh ammunition. Wrap it well with plastic wrap before assembling any outer adornments.

1 cup sifted cake flour
1½ cups granulated sugar
1¼ cups egg whites (10 to 12), at room temperature
1¼ teaspoons cream of tartar
¼ teaspoon salt
1 teaspoon vanilla extract
¼ teaspoon almond extract
¾ cup chocolate chips
Confectioners' sugar, for dusting

Preheat the oven to 325 degrees.

Sift the flour and ½ cup of the sugar together 4 times.

Beat the egg whites until foamy; add the cream of tartar and salt. Beat until moist peaks form when the beater is withdrawn.

Add the remaining sugar, 2 tablespoons at a time, beating thoroughly after each addition. Add the vanilla and almond extracts. Sift about ¼ cup of the flour-sugar mixture at a time over the meringue; fold in until no flour shows. Fold in the chocolate chips.

Turn into an ungreased tube pan and bake in the preheated oven until firm to the touch, about 1 hour. Invert the pan on a wire rack and allow the cake to cool completely in the pan. Unmold and dust with confectioners' sugar.

Mrs. Johnson's Coffee Cake

Serves 8 to 10

This is a concoction straight out of Bert Greene's childhood and the recipe has taken him a lifetime to get straight. The original was a standby of the Greenes' Swedish neighbor, who would whip the batter whenever her coffee percolator was on the stove. When the scent of the golden leavening assails his nostrils, Greene claims the past is recaptured—faster than he could chomp a madeleine! Give it with love (in a tin) for it keeps for a week.

8 tablespoons unsalted butter, softened
1¼ cups granulated sugar
2 eggs
4 tablespoons strong coffee
¾ teaspoon vanilla extract
2 cups sifted all-purpose flour
1 teaspoon baking powder
1 teaspoon baking soda
⅛ teaspoon salt
1¼ cups sour cream
¼ cup currants
½ cup packed dark brown sugar
⅓ cup finely chopped walnut meats
2 teaspoons ground cinnamon
2 teaspoons instant coffee powder
1 cup confectioners' sugar
½ teaspoon half-and-half

Cream the butter and granulated sugar in a large bowl. Beat in the eggs, one at a time. Stir in 1 tablespoon coffee and ½ teaspoon vanilla.

Mix together the flour, baking powder, baking soda and salt. Add the flour mixture, alternating with sour cream, to the butter mixture, beating gently after each addition.

Soak the currants in hot water to cover for 8 minutes; drain. Combine the currants, brown sugar, walnuts, cinnamon, and coffee powder in a bowl.

Preheat the oven to 375 degrees.

Spread one quarter of the reserved batter into the bottom of a well-buttered 12-cup bundt or tube pan. Sprinkle with one-third of the currant mixture. Repeat the layering, ending with batter. Bake in the preheated oven until a toothpick inserted in the center comes out clean, about 55 to 60 minutes. Cool on a rack for 20 minutes. Remove from pan and cool completely.

Combine the confectioners' sugar and half-and-half with the remaining 3 tablespoons coffee and ¼ teaspoon vanilla in a small bowl. Mix until smooth. Drizzle over the cake.

Golden Christmas Cake

When the holidays roll around, we dust off the recipe for this sunny yellow fruitcake (sans gooky candied fruits). This cake merely depends on orange and bits of crystallized pineapple for its extraordinary tincture. We generally give this in fruitcake tins, which are available at many gift and gourmet stores. You may even have some saved from previous gifts to you.

Butter, for greasing the pan
8 ounces unsalted butter, softened
1 cup superfine sugar
4 eggs
3⅔ cups sifted all-purpose flour
1 teaspoon baking powder
½ teaspoon salt
1½ cups buttermilk
1 teaspoon baking soda
Grated peel of 2 oranges
2 teaspoons vanilla extract
1 cup coarsely chopped pecans
½ cup shelled whole pistachio nuts
1 cup chopped dates
½ cup chopped crystallized pineapple
½ cup plus 1½ tablespoons orange juice
1 cup granulated sugar
¾ cup confectioners' sugar
3 tablespoons Grand Marnier liqueur

Preheat the oven to 325 degrees. Butter a 10-inch tube pan.

Beat the butter until light and fluffy in a large bowl; gradually beat in the superfine sugar. Beat in the eggs, one at a time, beating well after each addition.

Sift the flour, baking powder and salt together. Combine the buttermilk and baking soda. Using a wooden spoon, stir the flour mixture into the egg mixture in six parts, alternating with sixths of the buttermilk mixture; stir until thoroughly mixed (do not use an electric mixer because the batter might curdle). Stir in the orange peel, vanilla, pecans, pistachio nuts, dates and pineapple.

Spread the batter evenly in the prepared tube pan. Bake in the preheated oven until a toothpick inserted in the center comes out clean, about 1 hour and 25 to 30 minutes.

Combine ½ cup orange juice and granulated sugar in a saucepan and bring to a boil. Pierce the top of the cake all over with a fork; spoon the orange juice syrup over the cake. Let it stand in the pan on a wire rack for 2 hours; tilt the pan occasionally to distribute the syrup.

Unmold the cake and turn right side up on a serving plate. Combine confectioners' sugar, Grand Marnier and 1½ tablespoons orange juice in a small bowl; drizzle over cake.

Colorado Red Cake

The last cake (ablush for all the talk about it already) has celebrated every one of his birthdays for as long as Phillip Schulz can remember. It is called Colorado Red Cake, though its interpreter, Mildred Schulz, of Golden, Colorado, suspects it may have originated at the Waldorf Astoria Hotel around the turn of the century and migrated westward soon thereafter. Mildred Schulz, Phillip's mother, is a genius baker and cook whose handicraft has enriched every Greene book so far. Her Red Cake is another example of prime cooking for giving.

The easiest way to mail this cake long distance is to leave the layers (loosened) in their original cake pans. Wrap first in plastic and then in insulated mailing bags. Be sure to include explicit instructions for splitting layers—and a recipe for the frosting, of course.

FOR THE CAKE:
8 tablespoons unsalted butter, softened
1½ cups granulated sugar
2 eggs
¼ cup red food coloring
1 teaspoon vanilla
2 tablespoons cocoa
1 teaspoon salt
1 cup buttermilk
2¼ cups sifted cake flour
1 teaspoon baking soda
1 teaspoon cider vinegar

FOR THE ICING:
3 tablespoons all-purpose flour
1 cup milk
1 cup granulated sugar
8 ounces unsalted butter, softened
1 teaspoon vanilla extract

Preheat the oven to 350 degrees. Butter and flour 2 9-inch round cake pans.

To make the cake: Cream the butter with the sugar until light. Beat in the eggs, one at a time. Stir the food coloring with the vanilla and cocoa to form a smooth paste. Beat into the butter mixture. Combine the salt and buttermilk. Beat into the butter mixture in three parts, alternating with three parts flour. Combine the baking soda and vinegar. Stir into the cake mixture.

Pour the batter into the prepared cake pans. Bake in the preheated oven until a toothpick inserted in the center comes out clean, about 30 minutes. Cool on a wire rack for 20 minutes. Unmold. When the cake is completely cool, cut each layer in half to form 4 layers.

To make the icing: Combine the flour with the milk in a saucepan and cook over low heat, stirring, until thick; cool.

Cream the sugar and butter together until very light, about 5 minutes. Add the vanilla, and slowly stir, or mix in, the thickened milk mixture. Spread over each layer, sandwich together, then ice the side and top of the cake.

Lemon Coconut Wafers

Makes about 6 dozen

The gift of our friend Pat Powell, this treasured recipe was passed down from Pat's grandmother Hornor, who lived in Mount Holly, New Jersey, to Pat's mother, who passed it to Pat, who passed it to us. We pass it out at Christmas, but you need not wait for a special occasion to do so.

Butter, for greasing baking sheet
8 tablespoons unsalted butter, melted
1 cup granulated sugar
1 egg
1 cup sifted all-purpose flour
1 teaspoon baking powder
⅓ cup evaporated milk
3½-ounce can shredded coconut
½ teaspoon finely grated lemon rind
¾ teaspoon lemon juice

Preheat the oven to 350 degrees. Lightly butter a 10-by-15-inch baking sheet.

Beat the melted butter with the sugar in a large bowl until well mixed. Beat in the egg.

Sift the flour with the baking powder. Add to the batter in three parts, alternating with three parts evaporated milk. Stir in the coconut, lemon rind and lemon juice.

Drop the batter about 2 inches apart by small teaspoonfuls onto the prepared baking sheet. Bake in the preheated oven until golden, about 7 minutes. Cool the cookies completely on the pan before removing them with a spatula.

Cape Fear Lace Cookies

Makes about 2 dozen

The ultimate oatmeal cookie, this is also a gift from a friend. Rosalie Gwathmey brought this heirloom recipe from North Carolina many years ago. Children (of all ages) dote on these, because they're super-crunchy. Pack them in tins, each layer separated with lacy paper doilies.

Butter, to grease baking sheet
1 egg
½ teaspoon vanilla
8 tablespoons unsalted butter, melted
1 cup light brown sugar
2 cups uncooked rolled oats
½ cup walnut meats, chopped

Preheat the oven to 375 degrees. Line a 10-by-15-inch baking sheet with aluminum foil and butter it lightly.

Beat the egg and vanilla in the medium-sized bowl of an electric mixer. Slowly beat in the butter. Add the sugar and beat until smooth. Beat in the rolled oats on low speed. Stir in the walnuts.

Drop the batter by generous teaspoonfuls onto the foil-lined baking sheet, placing them far apart. There should be only 6 cookies on the sheet. Spread the cookie batter flat; do not mound. Bake in the preheated oven until golden brown, about 8 minutes. Remove the foil from the baking sheet, along with the cookies. Allow them to cool completely on a wire rack before peeling off the foil. Prepare another foil-lined sheetful of cookies and go on repeating the procedure until all the batter is used.

Benne Wafers

Makes about 2 dozen

Black cooks contributed most of the wondrous seasonings in Southern cuisine. In North Carolina, they claim that bennes (sesame seeds) were originally brought to the territory on slave ships for good luck. True or not, it was a lucky day when someone slipped the bennes into a cookie dough. These cookies keep well, so we ship them everywhere in plastic bags, tucked into antique ceramic teapots.

Butter, to grease baking sheet
1 egg
½ teaspoon vanilla
6 tablespoons unsalted butter, melted
¾ cup light brown sugar
¼ cup all-purpose flour
½ cup pecans, chopped
½ cup toasted sesame seeds

Preheat the oven to 400 degrees. Line a 10-by-15-inch baking sheet with aluminum foil and butter it lightly.

Beat the egg and vanilla in the medium-sized bowl of an electric mixer. Slowly beat in the butter. Add the sugar and beat until smooth. Beat in the flour on low speed in 3 parts. Stir in the pecans and sesame seeds.

Drop 6 teaspoonfuls of cookie batter onto the foil-lined sheet. Bake in the preheated oven until golden brown, 5 to 7 minutes. Remove the foil from the baking sheet along with the cookies. Allow them to cool completely on a wire rack before peeling off the foil. Prepare another foil-lined sheetful of cookies and continue to repeat the procedure until all the batter is used.

Rose's Almond Squares

Makes about 5 dozen

Rose Schweitzer, who used to co-own the Five Oaks restaurant in Greenwich Village, considered these special. "And special things should only be made for someone you love," she used to say. We pack these squares in a box tied with golden string, and decorate it with self-stick hearts . . . and flowers. Like a fresh rose tied in the center bow!

1 cup plus 2 tablespoons all-purpose flour
2 tablespoons confectioners' sugar
8 tablespoons unsalted butter, cut into bits
1½ cups brown sugar, packed
2 eggs, beaten
1 teaspoon almond extract
½ cup shredded coconut
¾ cup chopped almonds
Confectioners' sugar

Preheat the oven to 400 degrees.

Combine 1 cup flour, 2 tablespoons confectioners' sugar and the butter in a mixing bowl; blend well with a pastry blender. Butter a 9-by-14-inch cookie sheet. Pat the flour mixture evenly over the bottom of the sheet. Bake in the preheated oven for 10 mintues. Remove and allow to cool slightly.

Combine the brown sugar, 2 tablespoons flour, the eggs, almond extract, coconut and almonds in a bowl; mix thoroughly with your hands. Spread over the pre-baked crust; bake until a toothpick inserted comes out clean, 15 to 20 minutes. Sprinkle with confectioners' sugar. Let cool before cutting into 1-by-2-inch squares.

70 / COOKING FOR GIVING

Raspberry Jammies

Makes about 3 dozen filled cookies

These cookies are like little crispy sandwiches filled with jam. This recipe is a big favorite among kids. Need we add, of all ages! Plastic, see-through tubes make fun containers for these.

8 ounces unsalted butter, softened
½ cup granulated sugar
2 egg yolks
Rind of 1 lemon, finely grated
1 teaspoon vanilla extract
Pinch of salt
2½ cups plus 3 tablespoons all-purpose flour
Butter, to grease baking sheets
½ cup raspberry preserves
2 tablespoons orange juice
1 tablespoon Orange Liqueur (page 84)
½ teaspoon finely grated orange peel

Beat the butter in a large bowl until light and fluffy. Slowly add the sugar. Beat in the egg yolks, one at a time, beating thoroughly after each addition. Beat in the lemon rind, vanilla and salt.

Stir 2 cups flour into the cookie dough with a wooden spoon. Transfer to a lightly floured board; knead in the remaining flour until smooth. Chill dough for 1 hour.

Preheat the oven to 375 degrees.

Lightly butter 2 10-by-15-inch baking sheets.

Roll out the dough ¼ inch thick and cut into 1½-inch rounds. Place on baking sheets about 1 inch apart. Bake in the preheated oven until lightly browned, about 12 minutes. Cool on a wire rack.

Combine the raspberry preserves, orange juice, orange liqueur and orange peel in a small saucepan. Cook over moderate heat until slightly thickened, about 5 minutes.

Turn half the cookies bottom side up. Coat each piece with about ¾ teaspoon of the preserve mixture. Cover with the remaining cookies bottom side down.

Shortbread

Shortbread (from Scotland) is a cookie that men, women and children too, seem to adore whatever their ethnic origin. What makes this version so delicate, aside from butter, of course, is a smidgen of vanilla and orange peel, which makes the bread positively beatific. This recipe (of ours) was once presented to us as a gift, baked in a wonderful stoneware shortbread plate and embossed with a thistle in the center of every slice. It was a nifty notion for gift giving, and we pass it on, with love.

8 ounces unsalted butter, softened
½ cup granulated sugar
1 egg yolk
2 tablespoons whipping cream
1½ teaspoons vanilla extract
½ teaspoon grated orange peel
2½ cups all-purpose flour
½ cup rice flour
Cornmeal, for sprinkling baking sheet

Preheat the oven to 325 degrees.

Cream the butter with the sugar in a mixing bowl. Beat in the egg yolk. Add the cream, vanilla and orange peel; mix thoroughly.

Combine the flours and work them into the butter mixture with your fingers. Knead lightly and form the dough into a ball.

Invert a 9-inch round cake pan; butter and flour the underside of the pan. Press the dough ball onto the surface to form a smooth 9-inch circle. Sprinkle a baking sheet with cornmeal; invert the dough onto the sheet, loosening it from the cake pan with a metal spatula if necessary. Smooth the top and press the edges with the tines of a fork.

Bake in the preheated oven for 10 minutes. Remove from the oven and press the shortbread lightly in the center with a shortbread mold. (A decorative cutter or butter mold will work just as well.) Score the shortbread into 8 to 12 wedges around the pattern, using a pastry wheel or serrated knife. Return to the oven and bake until the edges begin to brown, about 40 minutes. Remove, and cool completely on a wire rack.

Candies

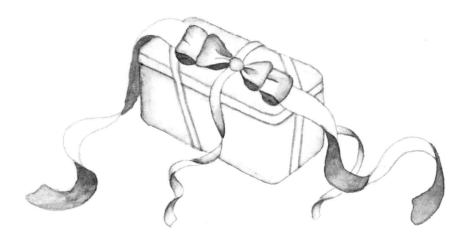

C andy-making in America is practically a lost art. Perhaps that is why we revere the few really good candy-makers of our acquaintance, and treasure their recipes so dearly.

As candy addicts, neither of us can resist the flavor of old-time goodness, as these recipes will surely make manifest. The crunch of true peanut brittle, the cosset of melting butterscotch and the comfort of deeply creamy chocolate fudge are never-to-be-forgotten childhood joys—and we exhort gift-givers everywhere to immediately rediscover them.

To our minds, candy is best packed in attractive containers with tight-fitting tops or in metal boxes with secure lids. Some of the most unusual we have discovered recently are tins that are molded and painted to resemble famous architectural sites (like the White House and the Plaza Hotel). New, these charming canisters look old and keep candy at its prime for a long time after the gift has been received. These tin boxes are made in England by Avon Tin of Bristol for Jack Cassidy & Associates Inc., U.S.A., and may be mail ordered for $7.00 (including postage) from Be Seated, 66 Greenwich Avenue, New York, NY 10011.

Peanut Brittle

Makes 2¼ pounds

The sweetest candy in our collection is itself a gift from the sweetest woman we know (and, in passing, one of the best cooks in the country), Mary Surina of San Pedro, California. Mary's talent is cooking for giving—and she does it with all her heart and damn the cholesterol and calories. Her magnificent peanut brittle is like no other the authors have ever eaten; pale golden to look at, it's heavenly on the tongue. Pack some in straw-covered cans with tight-fitting lids or reclaimed peanut butter jars.

3 cups raw shelled peanuts
1½ teaspoons baking soda
½ teaspoon salt
2 cups granulated sugar
1 cup light corn syrup
½ cup water
4 tablespoons unsalted butter

Preheat the oven to 350 degrees.

Spread the peanuts in a 10-by-15-inch pan. Bake in the oven for 15 minutes; remove and place in a bowl. Keep warm.

Combine the baking soda and salt; set aside. Combine the sugar, corn syrup and water in a medium-sized saucepan. Bring to a boil. Boil rapidly until the syrup begins to turn a golden color (275 degrees on a candy thermometer). Add the nuts and continue cooking, stirring often until the syrup is a clear gold color (295 degrees on a candy thermometer). Remove from the heat. Quickly stir in the butter-and-soda mixture. Immediately pour into the baking pan. Allow to cool for 2 hours. Break into pieces.

Mary's Toffee

Makes 2½ pounds

Another gift of love from Mary Surina of San Pedro, California. The authors were thrice the recipients of this heavenly chocolate-nut-toffee roka. Once, while we were visiting Mary, she pressed a goodly amount on us from her supply in the freezer. When we swooned, she sent a huge box as the crowning glory of her Christmas gifts. When we asked for the recipe for this book, it came by express mail. Speak of cooking for giving—there's no stopping our friend Mary!

1 cup coarsely chopped almonds
1 cup finely chopped almonds
8 ounces unsalted butter
1⅓ cups granulated sugar
1 tablespoon light corn syrup
3 tablespoons water
14 ounces milk chocolate,
**   melted**

Preheat the oven to 300 degrees.

Spread the 2 kinds of almonds in separate shallow pans and place in the oven until delicately browned, 10 to 12 minutes. Remove; keep warm.

Meanwhile, heat the butter in a medium-sized saucepan over low heat; add the sugar, corn syrup and water. Bring to a boil. Cook, stirring occasionally, until the mixture is a deep golden color (300 degrees on a candy thermometer). Quickly stir in the coarsely chopped almonds.

Pour mixture into an ungreased 9-by-13-inch pan; allow to cool thoroughly, about 1 hour. Turn the hardened and cooled mixture onto wax paper; spread the top with half of the melted chocolate and sprinkle evenly with half of the finely chopped almonds. Cover with wax paper and invert; spread the bottom with the remaining chocolate and sprinkle evenly with the remaining almonds. Place in the refrigerator until the chocolate is firm. Break into pieces.

Butter Pecan Turtles

Makes about 4½ dozen

This old-fashioned butterscotch-plus-chocolate bar was sent by Phillip Schulz's sister Jeanette Deschamps of Naperville, Illinois, as Christmas booty last year. The confection was so admired that it disappeared in half a day. Later poor Jeanette was besieged for the recipe. The original, it turns out, was once printed on a Land O'Lakes butter carton, but has undergone major alterations in the kitchens of Deschamps, Schulz and Greene. But no better (or sweeter) candy will you ever sample. We pack these between slip sheets of wax paper in a sturdy wooden box that travels well.

FOR THE CRUST:
2 cups all-purpose flour
1 cup brown sugar, packed
8 tablespoons unsalted butter,
  softened
1 cup pecan halves

FOR THE CARAMEL:
10½ tablespoons (5½ ounces)
  unsalted butter
½ cup brown sugar, packed

5-ounce bar of milk chocolate,
  cut into bits (about 1 cup)

Preheat the oven to 350 degrees.

To make the crust: Combine the flour, brown sugar and butter in a mixing bowl. Beat with an electric mixer until the mixture is fine, about 3 to 4 minutes. Pat firmly and evenly into the bottom of an ungreased 9-by-13-inch pan. Spread the pecan halves evenly over the crust.

To make the caramel: Combine the butter and brown sugar in a small saucepan. Bring to a boil over moderate heat, stirring constantly. Boil 1 minute while continuing to stir. Pour evenly over the crust. Bake until the caramel layer is bubbly and crust is golden, about 20 minutes.

Remove from the oven and immediately sprinkle the surface with chocolate bits. Allow the chocolate to melt slightly. Using the point of a knife, gently swirl chocolate as the pieces melt. Do not spread. Cool completely before cutting into 1½-inch squares.

Pecan Almond Fudge

The densest fudge in our sugary repertoire is a snap to whip together. Even a child can do it—and will, given the opportunity. The recipe is an old one, chock-a-block with chopped pecans, the way we like it, but instead of the obligatory vanilla, it is flavored with Amaretto, which makes a really different taste. We pack it into interestingly shaped cardboard boxes, layered with doilies and tied up with any number of frills and furbelows.

2 cups granulated sugar
1 cup light cream or half-and-half
2 ounces unsweetened chocolate
2 tablespoons unsalted butter
1 teaspoon Amaretto
1 cup chopped pecans

Combine the sugar, cream and chocolate in a medium-sized saucepan. Cook over moderate heat until the sugar dissolves and chocolate has melted. Raise the heat slightly and boil the mixture until it registers 238 degrees on a candy thermometer (or forms a ball when dropped into cold water). Remove from the heat and stir in the butter and Amaretto. Let stand 5 minutes.

Beat the mixture with a wooden spoon until it starts getting very thick. Fold in the pecans and pour into a buttered 8-inch-square cake pan. Let stand until cool and set before cutting into squares.

Shaved and Sugared Fruit Peels

Makes about 48 pieces

The last confection is a gift from our friend, Jacques Pépin, and has been only slightly amended in our kitchen. It is a shower of gold and glittery peels, delicately flavored with citrus and sugared to make a perfect after-dinner sweet to accompany strong black coffee. We pack these as gifts in glass apothecary jars—but you may be as creative as you wish. Sugared peels stay fresh in a cool spot for quite some time, and freeze nicely, packed in airtight plastic bags.

3 to 4 tangerines (or oranges) with bright shiny skins
1 large grapefruit
2 limes
2 lemons
3½ cups granulated sugar, plus extra for dusting the peels
Pinch of cinnamon

Make cuts through the skin of each piece of fruit with a sharp knife. Separate each into 6 sections. Separate the skin from the fruit and use the flat blade of the knife to scrape off the thin layer of bitter pith under the skin, approximately ¹/₁₆ inch deep.

Place the peels in a large saucepan and cover with cold water. Bring to a boil, boil 30 seconds, rinse under cold running water and drain.

Wipe out the saucepan with paper towels; return the peels and repeat the process. Drain and set aside.

Mash the juice from the remaining citrus pulp through a strainer. You should have about 1 cup liquid. Place the juice in a large saucepan. Add 3½ cups sugar and about 7 cups water. Bring to a boil; add the pinch of cinnamon and the reserved peels. Reduce the heat slightly; boil, uncovered, for about 1½ hours. The peels will be translucent at this point and the liquid will have turned into a thick syrup. Be careful not to burn the syrup as it thickens.

Using tongs, transfer the peels to a cookie sheet that is covered with about ½ inch sugar. As they cool, roll them in the sugar until they are well coated. Remove to a tray; allow to cool and harden in a dry place, for about 1 hour. Store the peels in an airtight metal box or sealed jar.

Fruits & Spirits

These days more and more Americans seem to prefer a dessert in a glass. And it is probably a sign of dietary concern as much as discretion that liqueurs and brandied fruits are replacing more conventional (and high caloric) sweets after dinner.

Fruit liqueurs and brandied fruits have been made and enjoyed therapeutically for centuries. But only recently has the making of them become part of the culinary do-it-yourself movement. And with good reason, for they are costly to buy, yet simple to whip up—for anyone with a jot of imagination, and spare closet room for the distillation period.

Procedures for fruited spirits are very basic. Alcohol (in most cases, vodka) is combined with a natural flavoring agent and allowed to steep for 10 days or longer. The liquor is then strained and judiciously sweetened. Straining removes the flavoring agent and also reveals a clear infusion. Coffee filters work admirably for this, although the process takes time. Several layers of cheesecloth may be used instead, but the liquid will need to be strained two or three times before it is bottled.

Spirited fruits are even simpler to prepare. The method requires fresh or dried fruit to be immersed in a syrup that is generously laced with alcohol, and then sealed. Because of their high alcoholic content, spirited fruits do not require any hot-water bath but do need time (ranging from several weeks to several months) for proper aging.

Investing in attractive decanters (for the spirits) and handsome glass airtight containers (for the fruits) will increase their value immeasurably as gifts. But make no mistake—everyone loves a boozy bequest!

Brandied Cherries

Makes 1½ pints

Greene's noteworthy grandmother always put up cherries and other ripe fruits in quart jars topped with healthy jiggers of spirituous liquor, and then let them steep for a month. She would serve this treat to her family along with homemade relish and pickles if she felt the Sunday-night meal of cold meats needed a jot of "perking up." More often, a jar was unsealed when some prized relatives from Cleveland appeared unexpectedly for dinner.

1½ quarts sour cherries
½ cup sugar
¼ teaspoon ground cinnamon
¼ cup water
Cognac

Pick the stems from the cherries and rinse them in cold water. Pack into sterilized jars.

Combine the sugar with the cinnamon in a small saucepan. Stir in the water. Place over moderate heat and stir until the sugar has dissolved. Divide the syrup among the jars. Add Cognac to cover the fruit. Seal. Store in a cool place, turning occasionally, for at least 1 month.

"Brandied" Plums

Makes about 5 pints

Both Greene and Schulz are assiduous collectors of old bottles and recipes. Some of the spiked fruits we prepare were culled from times past (a hundred-odd years ago) when brandy alone kept a plum in prime condition during a long cold winter. Pack yours, as we do, in old Mason jars or drugstore apothecary bottles with ground-glass stoppers.

2 quarts ripe plums
½ stick cinnamon bark (broken in half again)
1 cup granulated sugar
½ cup orange juice
⅛ teaspoon salt
2 whole cloves
¼ lemon, sliced paper-thin
Grand Marnier liqueur

Select plums that are ripe and juicy; wash and pack into sterilized jars. Add a piece of cinnamon bark to each jar.

Combine sugar, orange juice, salt and cloves in a saucepan. Bring to a boil; add the lemon slices and simmer until they become transparent.

Cover the plums halfway with the syrup, making sure each jar has a slice of lemon. Fill with Grand Marnier and seal.

Store in a cool dark place for 1 month. Turn the jars upside down once each week. The longer the plums stand, the better they taste when served.

Pears in Vodka

Makes 4 pints

These preserved pears are the easiest (and most welcome) gift on our liquorous agenda. The steeped fruit makes a zesty accompaniment to meats or fowl, or a fabled dessert when served with ice cream and a splash of the darkly rich chocolate sauce you will find on page 57. Neat gift idea: Give a lucky party a jar of both in tandem, wrapped in brown paper bags adorned with pairs of playing cards (two aces, two kings, two queens, etc.), plus a gift tag: "Have a pear on us!"

1 cup sugar
1¼ cups water
¼ teaspoon anise seed
5 firm ripe pears (about
2½ pounds)
1 pint vodka, approximately

Combine the sugar and water in a small saucepan. Cook over moderate heat until the sugar dissolves. Remove from the heat. Stir in the anise seed and let stand until cool.

Peel the pears, quarter them and remove their cores. Pack them into sterilized jars.

Divide the liquid evenly among the jars. Fill each jar with vodka. Seal. Let stand for at least 2 months before serving.

Plums in White Wine

Makes about 2½ pints

The plums are blue, the wine is white, and the resultant jar is ready before you know it. We preserve plums in wine year after year because they are always subtly requested by the bevy of put-up recipients. Tie your jars in sealed ceramic crocks with blue and white ribbons, please.

1½ pounds Italian blue plums
  (about 30 plums)
3 curls of orange rind about
  ½ inch wide and 3 inches long
1 cup sweet white wine
¼ cup orange juice
2 cups granulated sugar
1 small cinnamon stick

Wipe the fruit and slit one side of each plum, using a sharp knife, and remove the pit. Place about 12 pitted plums in each sterilized jar. Add a curl of orange rind.

Combine the wine, orange juice, sugar and cinnamon stick in a medium-sized saucepan. Bring to a boil; reduce heat. Simmer 15 minutes. Discard the cinnamon stick.

Pour into jars. Seal. Place in a hot-water bath for 20 minutes. Store in a cool place.

Peach Halves in Amaretto

Makes 2 pints

This is the ultimate "put-up" dessert gift—because it lasts on the shelf until the penultimate moment when a dessert has to be produced at once. Then, the halves of glistening fruit will happily adorn mounds of ice cream, meringues, or even lightly whipped cream—and the diner will be swept away, for the taste of these peaches is truly delectable.

5 unblemished ripe peaches
  about 1¼ pounds)
⅔ cup water
6 tablespoons sugar
⅓ cup Amaretto (approximately)

Plunge the peaches into boiling water for about 30 seconds to loosen the skins. Drain. Cool. Carefully remove the skins, taking care not to damage the peaches. Cut in halves; discard the pits.

Divide the peach halves between two sterilized pint jars.

Combine the water with sugar in a small saucepan. Bring to a boil; remove from heat. Cool slightly and pour over peaches. The liquid should come about halfway up the jar. Add enough Amaretto to each jar to cover the peaches. Seal. Place in a hot-water bath for 20 minutes. Store in a cool place.

Prunes and Currants in Hazelnut Liqueur

Makes 1 pint

The best last-minute gifts in our admittedly narrow view are prepared fast—out of ingredients practically any kitchen cupboard will yield readily. Take the lowly prune, for example. Combining this fruit with dried currants and a tot of liqueur (plus a little corn syrup) will invest an everyday staple with the grandeur of a great homemade. Best of all, it requires no cooking time whatsoever. A hot-water bath and a stay in a cool place does the work!

½ pound dried prunes
½ cup dried currants
1 3-inch curl lemon rind
1 stick cinnamon
½ cup light corn syrup
½ cup hazelnut liqueur

Place the prunes and currants in a sterilized jar. Add the lemon curl and cinnamon stick. Add the corn syrup. Add enough liqueur to cover the dried fruit. Seal. Place in a hot-water bath for 15 minutes. Store in a cool place, turning occasionally, for at least 3 weeks.

Dried Apricots in Coconut Liqueur

Makes 3 half-pints

Yet another instant put-up! The amazing aspect of these spiked dried fruits is the way they change and take on a new guise (and flavor) after a spirit bath. The apricots in question make a fine accompaniment to a curried dinner, or can grace a platter of roast meat when the other pickings seem slim. We preserve fruits in wide-mouthed glass jars with brightly colored plastic screw top lids—and always note some serving ideas on an accompanying gift card.

11-ounce package dried apricots
3 4-inch curls orange rind
¾ cup light corn syrup
¾ cup coconut-rum liqueur

Divide the apricots among 3 ½-pint sterilized jars. Add an orange curl to each jar. Add ¼ cup corn syrup to each jar. Add enough liqueur to each jar to cover the apricots. Seal. Place in a hot-water bath for 15 minutes. Store in a cool place, turning occasionally, for at least 3 weeks.

Anise Liqueur

Anise is said to be nature's favorite flavor—think of fennel, chervil, tarragon and licorice, for a start—and the best uses for anise are all, happily, alcoholic. This recipe makes a lively yet smooth liqueur which should never be wasted on seasoning a cup of espresso. For licorice lovers, package this infusion in a tissue-wrapped bottle tied with licorice ropes.

1 teaspoon sesame seeds
3 tablespoons anise seeds
3 cups vodka
1¼ cups sugar
1 cup water

Combine the sesame and anise seeds in a quart jar. Add the vodka. Cover the jar tightly. Let stand for 10 days, shaking the jar occasionally. Strain.

Combine the sugar and water in a saucepan. Bring to a boil, stirring to dissolve the sugar. Boil for 2 minutes and remove from the heat. Let stand for 10 minutes. Combine the syrup with the liqueur and bottle it. Age for 10 days before giving.

Café au Rhum

A smidgen of vanilla and a splash of rum give this coffee liqueur its special bouquet. Tell the lucky recipients to try it in Irish Coffee or simply "on the rocks" with a teaspoon of heavy cream floated on top. Using freeze-dried coffee is a quick (and potent) way to make this, but any extra-strong brewed coffee will do as well. Give this liqueur in a glass decanter, or tied to a pair of demitasse cups.

2 cups sugar
1 cup water
1-inch piece of vanilla bean
3 tablespoons freeze-dried coffee
½ cup boiling water
1½ cups vodka
½ cup golden rum

Combine the sugar with the water and vanilla bean in a saucepan. Simmer over medium-low heat for 20 minutes. Remove from the heat. Let stand for 10 minutes.

Combine the freeze-dried coffee with the boiling water. Add to the sugar-vanilla mixture. Then add the vodka and rum. Cool completely.

Pour the mixture into a quart jar and let it stand for at least 10 days. Strain and bottle it.

Walnut Liqueur

Makes 1 quart

Walnuts make the most unusual liqueur in the world. The best we ever sampled came from the Balkans, where the process is arduous and the steeping takes years. Ours is a somewhat modified version; not so sweet, and with a shorter distillation period. It takes a full month to ripen this infusion, but it is, we guarantee, well worth the wait. Package your decanter of cordial inside a box of unshelled walnuts and tie a jaunty nut-cracker to the bow!

**1 pound walnuts in their shells,
   lightly crushed
Boiling water to cover
3-inch piece of vanilla bean
4 allspice berries
4½ cups vodka
¾ cup sugar
¼ cup water**

Cover the crushed walnuts in their shells with boiling water. Let stand for 10 minutes, then drain.

Combine the walnuts with the vanilla bean and allspice berries in a 2-quart jar. Add the vodka and cover the jar tightly. Let stand for 4 weeks, shaking the jar occasionally. Strain.

Combine the sugar and water in a saucepan. Bring the mixture to a boil, stirring to dissolve the sugar. Boil for 2 minutes and then remove from the heat. Let stand for 10 minutes. Combine this mixture with the liqueur and bottle it. Allow to age at least 10 days before giving.

Orange Liqueur

Makes 1 quart

Perhaps the most widely used liqueur in the world, this version tastes like Curaçao and is twice as tasty in cooking as it is over ice. We always make it "twice up" as well. One bottle, raffia-wrapped, to give—and one bottle, unadorned, to flavor the stew.

**4 large oranges
2-inch piece vanilla bean
2 cups vodka
1 cup brandy
1 cup granulated sugar
1 cup water**

Remove the zest (the orange part of the peel only) from the oranges and put it in a quart jar with the vanilla bean. Add the vodka and brandy. Cover the jar tightly. Let stand 10 days, shaking the jar occasionally. Strain.

Combine the sugar and water in a saucepan. Bring the mixture to a boil, stirring to dissolve the sugar. Boil for 2 minutes and then remove from the heat. Let stand for 10 minutes. Combine this mixture with the liqueur and bottle it.

Allow this liqueur to age for at least 10 days before giving.